DESIGN

BASICS

Fourth Edition

DESIGN

BASICS

DAVID A. LAUER

STEPHEN PENTAK

The Ohio State University

HARCOURT BRACE COLLEGE PUBLISHERS

*Fort Worth Philadelphia San Diego New York Orlando Austin San Antonio
Toronto Montreal London Sydney Tokyo*

For Ernie
D.A.L.

For Debbie
S.P.

Publisher	TED BUCHHOLZ
Acquisitions Editor	BARBARA J. C. ROSENBERG
Developmental Editor	TERRI HOUSE
Project Editor	JEFF BECKHAM
Senior Production Manager	KATHLEEN FERGUSON
Art Director	NICK WELCH
Photo Researcher	JOELLE BURROWS

Cover image by Jack Zeman, Dallas

COPYRIGHT © 1995, 1985, 1979 BY HARCOURT BRACE & COMPANY
COPYRIGHT © 1990 BY HOLT, RINEHART AND WINSTON, INC.

ADDRESS FOR EDITORIAL CORRESPONDENCE: HARCOURT BRACE COLLEGE PUBLISHERS,
301 COMMERCE STREET, SUITE 3700, FORT WORTH, TX 76102.

ADDRESS FOR ORDERS: HARCOURT BRACE & COMPANY, 6277 SEA HARBOR DRIVE,
ORLANDO, FL 32887. 1-800-782-4479, OR 1-800-433-0001 (IN FLORIDA).

PRINTED IN THE UNITED STATES OF AMERICA

ISBN: 0-15-501184-7

LIBRARY OF CONGRESS CATALOG CARD NUMBER: 93-80822

890123 048 987

PREFACE

The fourth edition of *Design Basics* continues to offer a modular format that allows instructors to select their own sequence of topics as they introduce students to the elements and principles of design. This is an ideal format for those who may read this book on their own and wish to use it as a reference. Although the modular structure remains, much has been revised and refined in this new edition. Furthermore, I am pleased and honored to join David Lauer as his co-author of the fourth edition. I have used all three previous editions.

Our challenge was to improve an already well-conceived text and to respond to the evolving requirements of an audience interested in visual language. The thoughtful comments of instructors who have used the book revealed areas for change and development.

More than half of the images contained in this edition are new, and with those changes there is an even greater diversity in sources. The artworks and designs of women, people of color, and a variety of cultures are better represented and this diversity of imagery includes artworks from many periods and places. The inclusive nature of this collection of art and design images is in keeping with the fundamental spirit of the book—that the elements and principles of design can be found in the significant works of all cultures and that they transcend the rich differences of media, imagery, time, place, and other factors.

The processes behind successful design solutions are as rich and varied as are the final products. Historical and cultural contexts join with individual vision to account for this variety. Chapter 1, Design Process, has been revised to include more evidence of the working process with examples of sources, influences, and the sketches that contribute to the final form of an artwork or design.

Each new edition of *Design Basics* has sought to bring greater clarity to the complex subject of color. This edition includes new images to illustrate the phenomena of color interaction, as well as useful information based on the Munsell Color System. New examples or artworks were selected to best illustrate the connections between color theory and practice.

Changes have also been introduced to make the book easier to use. Key terms are now presented in bold type, and are defined in the new glossary.

Design Basics attempts to present a demystifying look at the elements, principles, and processes of design in clear accessible language. We hope this new edition conveys the spirit and methods of visual invention as expressed by Josef Albers:

> To design is
> to plan and organize
> to order and relate
> and to control.
> In short it embraces
> all means opposing
> disorder and accident.
> There it signifies
> a human need
> and qualifies man's
> thinking and doing.

ACKNOWLEDGMENTS

Art and design are often the result of collaboration, and this is the case for this textbook as well. Editors and researchers contribute to the project and their efforts are appreciated. Special thanks are due to Stacy Clause, who assisted in researching new images, and to Sean Foley, who wrote the glossary. We are also grateful to the reviewers who provided so many good and useful suggestions:

Sandra Rowe
California State Polytechnic University

Mary Witte
Boise State University

William C. Zwingleberg
Catonsville Community College

Sharon Eckstein
Western Michigan University

Glenn Dunlap
Indiana State University

Susan Moss
Fort Lewis College

Judith Bell
California State University, Fullerton

Pamela Lowrie
College of DuPage

Patrick Shuck
Saint Louis Community College

Cynthia M. Kukla
Illinois State University

S.P.

CONTENTS

DESIGN BASICS

1

DESIGN PROCESS

INTRODUCTION

de-sign (di zīn′) *v.t.* 1. to prepare the preliminary sketch or the plans for (a work to be executed) esp. to plan the form and structure of: *to design a new bridge.* 2. to plan and fashion artistically or skillfully . . .

The dictionary goes on to give sixteen more definitions and usages for the word "design." Obviously this common word has many applications. But in all of these definitions there is one common element: the word "plan" appears over and over. To *design* indeed means to *plan,* to *organize* **(A)**. Design is essentially the opposite of chance. In ordinary conversation, when we say "it happened by design" we mean something was planned and did not occur just by accident. People in all occupations plan, but the artist or designer is someone who plans the arrangement of elements to form a *visual* pattern. Depending on the field, these "elements" will vary—all the way from painted symbols to written words to scenic flats to bowls to furniture to windows and doors. But the result is always a *visual* organization. Art, like other careers and occupations, is concerned with seeking answers to problems. Art, however, seeks visual solutions in what is often called the *design process.*

The arts are called "creative" fields because there are no predetermined correct answers to the problems. Infinite variations in individual interpretations and applications are possible. Problems in art vary in specifics and complexity and take various forms. Independent painters or sculptors usually create their own problems or avenues they wish to explore. These may be as wide or as narrow as the artist chooses. The architect or graphic and industrial designer is usually *given* the problem, often with very specific options and clearly defined limitations. Students in art classes also usually are in this category—they execute a series of assignments devised by the instructor and requiring rather specific solutions. However, all art or visual problems are similar in that a creative solution is desired.

We use the word "creative" to mean a solution that is original, imaginative, fresh, or unusual. The poster in **B** is a wonderful expression of the creative approach. It is a simple design that graphically shows an important idea. Knowing *how* to do something is not necessarily the essential factor: it is knowing *what* to do. The ability to know what to reject (or erase) is as important as simply having the talent to create something. The circular pencil shows that *both* its ends are vital to this design process.

The creative aspect of art also includes the often-heard phrase that "there are no rules in art." This is true. In solving problems visually, there is no list of strict or absolute *dos* and *don'ts* to follow. Given all the varied objectives of visual art through the ages, definite laws are impossible. However, the "no rules" phrase may seem to imply that all designs are equally valid and visually successful. This is not true. Artistic practices and criteria have been developed from successful works, of which an artist or designer should be aware. Thus, guidelines (*not* rules) exist that usually will assist in the creation of successful designs. These guidelines certainly do not mean that the artist is limited to any specific solution.

Discussions of art often distinguish between two aspects, **content** and **form**. *Content* implies the subject matter, story, or information that the artwork seeks to communicate to the viewer. *Form* is the purely visual aspect, the manipulation of the various elements and principles of design. Content is what artists want to say; form is how they say it. Problems in art can concern one or both categories.

Sometimes the aim of a work of art is purely aesthetic. Subject matter can be absent and the problem related only to creating visual pleasure. Purely abstract adornment or decoration is a very legitimate role in art. Very often, however, problems in art have a purpose beyond mere visual satisfaction. Art is, and always has been, a means of visual communication.

A

A *It's Time to Get Organized.* 1986. Poster. John Kuchera, Art Director and Designer; Hutchins/Y&R.
B Poster for the School of Visual Arts. 1978. Designer: Tony Palladino. Courtesy of School of Visual Arts.

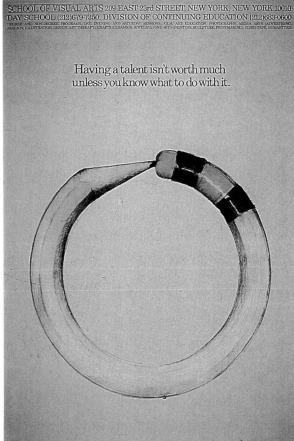

B

INTRODUCTION

We have all heard the cliché "a picture is worth a thousand words." This is true. There is no way to calculate how much each of us has learned through pictures. Communication has always been an essential role for art. Written communication indeed can be traced back to when "writing" was done simply in pictorial symbols rather than letters. Today, pictures can function as a sort of international language. A picture can be understood when written words may be unintelligible to the foreigner or the nonliterate. We do not need to understand German to grasp immediately that the message of the poster in **A** is pain, suffering, and torture.

In art, as in communication, the artist or designer is *saying* something to the viewer. Here the successful solution not only is visually effective but also communicates an idea. Any of the elements of art can be used in communication. Purely abstract lines, color, and shapes can be very effective in expressing ideas or feelings. Many times communication is achieved through symbols, pictorial images that suggest to the viewer the theme or message. The ingenuity of creative imagination exercised in selecting these images can be important in the finished work's success.

In art, as in communication, images are frequently combined with written words. The advertisements we see every day usually use both elements, coordinated to reinforce the design's purpose.

Countless paintings demonstrate that words are not a necessity for communication: two examples are shown that suggest the idea of movement or change. In *Dog on a Leash* **(B)** we instantly feel the motion taking place. No words are needed to communicate the idea. In **C** the visual and intellectual are combined. We *read* the word, but the letter repetition and placement also visually suggest the idea of motion.

These successful design solutions are due, of course, to good ideas. "How do I get an idea?" is a question often heard from students. Actually almost everyone shares this dilemma from time to time. Even the professional artist can stare at the empty canvas, the successful writer at the blank page. An idea in art can take many forms, varying from a specific visual effect to an intellectual communication of a definite message. Ideas encompass both the areas of content and form.

It is doubtful that anyone can truly explain why or how an idea suddenly arises. While doing one thing, we can be thinking about something else. Our ideas can occur when we are in the shower, mowing the lawn, or in countless other seemingly unlikely situations. An answer to what we have been puzzling over can appear "out of the blue." But we need not be concerned here with sudden solutions. They will continue to happen, but is that the only procedure? The relevant question is, "What can we do consciously to stimulate this creative process?" What sort of activities can promote the likelihood that a solution to a problem will present itself?

Many people today are concerned with such questions. There has been a great deal of study of the "creative process," and a number of worthwhile books and articles have been devoted to it, featuring numerous technical terms to describe aspects of this admittedly complex subject. But let me suggest three very simple activities with very simple names.

Thinking

Looking

Doing

These activities are *not* sequential steps and certainly not independent procedures. They overlap and may be accomplished almost simultaneously or by jumping back and forth from one to another. Individuals vary; people are not programmed machines in which rigid step-by-step procedures lead inevitably to answers; people's feelings and intuitions may assist in making decisions. Problems vary so that a specific assignment may immediately suggest an initial emphasis on one of these suggestions. But all three procedures can stimulate the artistic problem-solving process.

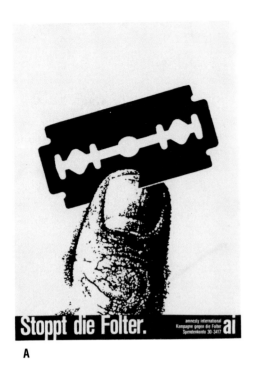

A

B

C

A *Stop Torture.* 1985. Poster for Amnesty International. Stephan Bundi, Art Director and Designer; Atelier Bundi, Bern, Switzerland.

B Giacomo Balla. *Dynamism of a Dog on a Leash.* 1912. Oil on canvas, 35⅜ × 43¼″ (90 × 110 cm). Albright-Knox Art Gallery, Buffalo, New York (bequest of A. Conger Goodyear and George F. Goodyear, 1964).

C The graphic technique matches the word's meaning to convey the idea.

PROCEDURES

THINKING

The well-known French artist Georges Braque wrote in his *Cahiers* (notebooks) that "one must not *think up* a picture." His point is valid; a painting is often a long process that should not be forced or created by formulas to order. However, each day countless designers must indeed "think up" solutions to design problems; *thinking* is an essential part of this solution. When confronted by a problem in any aspect of life, the usual first step is to think about it. Thinking is applicable also to art and visual problems. It is involved in all aspects of the creative process. Every step in creating a design involves choices, and the selections are determined by thinking. Chance or accident is also an element in art. But art cannot be created mindlessly, although some twentieth-century art movements have attempted to eliminate rational thought as a factor in creating art and to stress intuitive or subconscious thought. But even then it is thinking that decides whether the spontaneously created result is worthwhile or acceptable. To say that "thinking" is somehow outside the artistic process is truly illogical.

Knowing what you are doing must precede your doing it. So thinking starts with understanding the problem at hand:

Precisely what is to be achieved? (What specific visual and/ or intellectual effect is desired?)

Are there visual stylistic requirements (illustrative, abstraction, nonobjective, and so on)?

What physical limitations (size, color, media, and so on) are imposed?

When is the solution needed?

These questions may all seem self-evident, but effort spent on solutions outside the range of these specifications will not be productive. "Failures" can occur simply because the problem was not fully understood at the very beginning.

Thinking can be especially important in art that has a specific theme or message. How can the concept be communicated in visual terms? A first step is to think logically of which images or pictures could represent this theme and to list them, or, better yet, sketch them quickly, since a visual answer is what you're seeking. Let's take a specific example: What could visually represent the idea of art or design? Some obvious symbols are shown in the designs on these pages, and you will easily think of more. You might expand the idea by discussing it with others. They may offer suggestions you have not considered. Professional designers often are assisted by reports from market surveys that reveal the ideas of vast numbers of people.

Sketch your ideas to see immediately the visual potential. At this point you do not necessarily decide on *one* idea. But it's better to narrow a broad list to a few ideas worthy of development. Choosing a visual symbol is only the first step. How will you use your choice? The examples shown use only very obvious symbols for art, but in an original and unexpected way:

a farmer grows a crop of lovely flowers by plowing with a *pencil*? **(A)**

a body-builder weightlifts a *brush*? **(B)**

These designs are imaginative and eye-catching. The symbol was just the first step. *How* that symbol was used provided the unique and successful solution.

Selecting a particular symbol may depend on limitations of size, medium, color, and so on. Even thinking of the future viewers may be an influence. To whom is this visual message addressed? What reaction do you want from this audience? What effect or feeling do you wish to create? To symbolize *art* as a bearded figure in a spattered smock and beret could be humorously effective in some situations while silly or trivial in others. Undoubtedly, none of these designs would be appropriate for a serious treatise on aesthetics.

A *Open House at Art Center.* 1988. Poster invitation for Art Center, Pasadena. Richard Louderback, Designer.
B Craig Coughlin. *Untitled.* 1993. Oil wash on paper, 11 × 17″ (28 × 43 cm). © Craig Coughlin.

Sunday, February 28, 1988
10:00 AM—4:00 PM: Explore the
campus and talk with faculty about:
Advertising, Environmental
Design, Film, Fine Arts, Illustration,
Industrial Design, Graphic and
Packaging Design, and Photo-
graphy. 10:30 AM: Welcome and
Orientation. 11:30 AM: Admissions
Seminar. 1:00 PM: Presentation on
Careers in the Visual Arts—Peggy
Van Pelt, Talent Development
Specialist, Disney Imagineering.
2:30 PM: Financial Aid Seminar.
3:00 PM: Seminar on Careers.

Open House
at Art Center
Sunday, February 28

Art Center offers the B.F.A., B.S.,
M.F.A. and M.S. degrees. Applications accepted for Summer, Fall
and Spring semesters.

For more information on the
Open House, call the Admissions
Office at (818) 584-5035.

Art Center College of Design,
1700 Lida Street,
Pasadena, California 91103.

ArtCenter

A

B

THINKING

FORM AND CONTENT

What shall be presented, and *how* will it be presented? The thinking stage of the design process is often a contest to define this relationship of form and content. The contest may play itself out in additions and subtractions as a painting is revised, or in the drafts and sketches of an evolving design concept. The solution may be found intuitively, or be influenced by cultural values, previous art, or the expectations of clients.

Raymond Loewy's revised logo for the Greyhound Bus Company is an example of content being clearly communicated by the appropriate image or form. The existing logo in 1933 **(A)** looked fat to Loewy, and the chief executive at Greyhound agreed. His revised version **(B)** (based on a thoroughbred greyhound) conveys the concept of speed and was accepted as the new logo.

Communication is least ambiguous when the relationship between form and content is clear and uncluttered. This is true of both images and objects. When such clarity is achieved we say that form follows function. In this case form is determined by content and function is a priority. This relationship is often easiest to see and acknowledge in utilitarian design, such as the furniture design of the American Shaker movement. The interior presented in **C** reveals a simple straightforward attitude toward furniture and space design. All of the furnishings are functional and free from extraneous decoration. The ladder back of the chair exhibits a second utility when it is hung on the rail. Everything in this space communicates the Shaker value of simplicity.

Peter Eisenman's Wexner Center for the Arts at The Ohio State University **(D)** is a **site specific** architectural design solution which takes into account the history of the setting and the context of the surrounding campus plan. The solution for the form of this art center was influenced by these factors. Eisenman's design includes brick tower structures reminiscent of a former armory building that was a campus landmark on this site. These new towers act as a visual reminder of the past integrated into an institution that has a mission to respond to art of the present.

The form an artist selects can also contradict the usual function in order to challenge the concepts of an audience. Edgar Heap of Birds presents just such a contradiction of our expectations for printed words. The word ''Sooners'' (the name given to the early white settlers of Oklahoma) is presented backward in the billboard shown in **E**. This is an immediate signal that something is wrong, whether or not we know the specific history.

Form and content issues would certainly be easier to summarize in a monocultural society. Specific symbols may lose meaning when they cross national, ethnic, or religious borders. Given these obstacles to understanding, it is a powerful testimony to the meaning inherent in form that artworks often communicate successfully across time and distance.

A

B

A Raymond Loewy. Original logo for Greyhound Bus Co.
B Raymond Loewy. Redesigned logo, 1933.
C Shaker interior. Reproduced by permission of the American Museum in Britain, Bath ©.
D Peter Eisenman. Wexner Center for the Arts, Ohio State University, Columbus. 1989.
E Hachivi Edgar Heap of Birds. *Apartheid Oklahoma.* 1989. Billboard, 5 × 10′ (13 × 25 cm). © Edgar Heap of Birds.

C

D

E

A Henry Moore. *Standing Figure.* 1962. Bronze, height 112″ (2.84 m).

B Henry Moore's collection of bones. © The Henry Moore Foundation.

C Jennifer Bartlett. *In the Garden Drawing #64.* 1980. Pencil on paper, 26 × 19½″ (66 × 49.5 cm). Courtesy Paula Cooper Gallery, New York.

D Jennifer Bartlett. *Study for In the Garden* (detail: 54 of 270 squares). 1980. Pencil, ink, gouache on paper, 24 × 36″ (61 × 91 cm). Commission, Institute for Scientific Information, Philadelphia. Collection of the artist; courtesy Paula Cooper Gallery, New York.

A

B

LOOKING

SOURCES

Looking is probably the primary education of any artist. This process of looking includes an observation both of nature and of human artifacts, including art, design, and commonplace objects. Most artists are stimulated by the visual world around them and learn of possibilities for expression by observing other art. Studying art from all periods, regions, and cultures enlightens you to a wealth of visual creations, better equipping you to discover your own solutions.

For better or worse we do not create our design solutions in an information vacuum. We have the benefit of an abundance of visual information coming at us through a variety of media, from books to television. On the plus side, we are treated to images one would previously have had to travel to see. On the minus side, it is easy to overlook that we are often seeing a limited (or altered) aspect of the original artwork by the time we see it in reproduction.

Sources in nature and culture are clearly identifiable in the works of some artists, while sources are less obvious in the works of others, perhaps only revealed when we see drawings or preparatory work. In any case a distinction should be made between **source** and **subject.** The source is a stimulus for an image or idea. For example, a bone can be the source for a work of sculpture. The subject, as mentioned previously, is tied to the content of the work, or the artist's ideas and way of seeing.

The sculptor Henry Moore noted that he had a tendency to pick up shells at the beach that resembled his current work in progress. In that way he recognized in nature a resemblance to forms he was already exploring in the studio. His sculpture of a mother embracing a child, for example, resembled the protective wrapping form of a broken shell he found. In turn the forms from nature he collected came to suggest possibilities for new figurative pieces. Moore's *Standing Figure* **(A)** bears a resemblance to various bones in his collection **(B)**, but is not a copy of any of them.

Jennifer Bartlett's series entitled *In the Garden* consists of dozens of works in a variety of media, including drawings such as **C** and mixed media studies such as **D**. The source of imagery is clearly a garden pool. The subject is the many ways of seeing the garden and thinking about painting. A variety of styles are presented in this series, which reflects both the process of looking at the original source and looking at art from various periods.

C

D

LOOKING

SOURCES

The art of looking is not entirely innocent. Long before the training in seeing we get in art and design classes, we are trained from an early age by our exposure to mass media. The images of TV, film, and print influence our self-image and our personal relationships. The distinction between "news" and "docudrama" is often a blurry one, and we have all heard someone exclaim "it was so real . . . it was like a movie!"

At times it seems that visual training demands a retraining of looking on slower, more conscious terms. "Look again," and "see the relationships" are often heard in a beginning drawing class. Part of this looking process is examining works of art and considering the images of mass media that shape our culture. Many artists actively address these issues in their art by using familiar images or quoting past artworks. While this may seem like an esoteric exercise to the beginning student, an awareness of the power of familiar images is fundamental to understanding visual communication.

Certain so-called "high art" images manage to become commonly known, or **vernacular,** through frequent reproduction. In the case of a painting like *Washington Crossing the Delaware* the image is almost as universally recognized as a religious icon once was. There is a long tradition of artists paying homage to the masters, and we can understand how an artist might study this or other paintings in an attempt to learn techniques. However, *George Washington Carver Crossing the Delaware* **(A)**, by the African-American artist Robert Colescott, strikes a different relationship to the well-known painting we recognize as a source. Colescott plays with the familiarity of this patriotic image and startles us with a presentation of negative black stereotypes. One American stereotype is overlaid on top of another, leading the viewer to confront preconceptions about both.

Andy Warhol gave back to a twentieth-century audience the familiar labels of everyday products. *Various Boxes* **(B)** is just such a presentation (or more accurately *representation* screen printed on wood). The very fact that we so easily recognize these product labels reveals the impact they have on our memory and imagination. It has been noted that what a viewer gets from an art piece is a reflection of what he or she brings to it. Looking, then, is clearly influenced by commercial images, which are as real a part of our lives as the elements of nature.

Looking is a complex blend of conscious searching and visual recollections. This searching includes looking at art, nature, and the vernacular images from the world around us, as well as formal research into new or unfamiliar subjects. What we hope to find are the elements that shape our own visual language.

A Robert Colescott. *George Washington Carver Crossing the Delaware*. 1975. Acrylic on canvas, 54 × 108″ (1.4 × 2.7 m). Phyllis Kind Gallery, New York and Chicago.
B Andy Warhol. *Various Boxes*. 1964. Silkscreen on wood; single box: 17⅛ × 17⅛ × 14″ (44 × 44 × 36 cm). © 1993 The Andy Warhol Foundation for the Visual Arts, Inc.

A

B

A

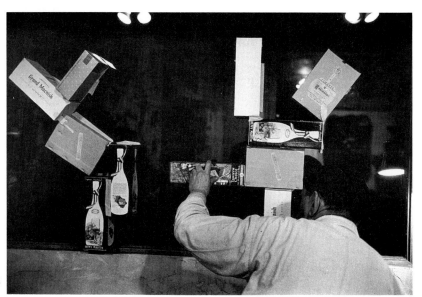

B

C

DOING

Doing starts with visual experimentation. For most artists and designers this is thinking with the materials. Trial and error, intuition, or deliberate application of a system are set into motion. At this point an idea starts to take form, whether in a sketch or in final materials. The artist Eva Hesse got right to the point with her observation on materials:

> 2 points of view—
> a) materials lifeless til given shape by creator
> b) materials by their own potential created their end

The work of Eva Hesse was known for embracing apparent contradictions. The studio view **(A)** presents a number of her sculptural works that embody both of the above points of view. Materials such as papier mâché, cloth, and wood were given shape by Hesse. There are also elements, such as the hanging, looping, and connecting ropes and cords, that reflect the inherent potential of the materials.

Photographs of the sculptor David Smith at work **(B)** show the playful side of doing. We can see the degree to which he allowed the materials to create their own end. Just as a child might delight in building blocks becoming a castle, Smith let the forms of cardboard boxes define the proportions of sculpture he would later complete in steel **(C)**. Smith stacked the boxes on a window sill and taped them to the window as he assembled each study. The influence of the window as a support shows through in the predominantly two-dimensional composition of the final pieces.

When designers leave a record of their drawings, we are able in effect to see them doing their work. This is the case with the construction drawings for Loewy's logo design **(D)**. The four steps depicted lay out the defining geometry of the scallop shell, and the first step shows that a circle provides the underlying form. These four drawings provide the map to the final version **(E)**, but undoubtedly other possibilities were explored before this one was settled on. Today, drawings such as these would probably be done on a computer, which can greatly speed up the viewing of alternate possibilities.

The doing step in the process obviously involves continuous looking and thinking, yet more than one artist, writer, or composer has observed that doing takes over with a life of its own. An artwork takes shape through you, and as it does you may find yourself wondering where the time went or what you were thinking of when a work session ends. This experience is exhilarating but includes the elements of risk and failure.

A wonderful film of the painter Philip Guston at work ends with him covering over his picture with white to begin again. Guston accepted such a setback along the way as normal and even necessary. His experience told him that revision would allow an idea to grow beyond an obvious or familiar starting point.

A Eva Hesse Studio, 1966. Installation photograph by Gretchen Lambert. © The Estate of Eva Hesse. All rights reserved.
B David Smith assembling liquor boxes as models for his sculptures.
C David Smith with completed sculptures *Cubi IV* and *Cubi V.*
D Raymond Loewy. Steps in the development of a new Shell logo, 1971.
E Raymond Loewy. Revision of Shell logo, 1971.

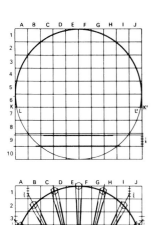
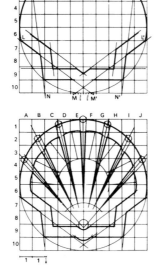

D

E

2

UNITY

INTRODUCTION

Unity, the presentation of an integrated image, is perhaps as close to a ''rule'' as art can approach. Unity means that a congruity or agreement exists among the elements in a design; they *look* as though they belong together, as though some visual connection beyond mere chance has caused them to come together. Another term for the same idea is **harmony.** If the various elements are not harmonious, if they appear separate or unrelated, your pattern falls apart and lacks unity.

Example **A** illustrates the idea of a high degree of unity. When we look at the elements in this design, we immediately see that they are all somewhat similar. This harmony or unity is not merely from our recognizing all of these items as pinball machines. Unity is achieved through a *visual* similarity between rectangular shapes and the repetition of other geometric patterns. The **negative shapes** or spaces between the forms are also similar and repeated. Such a unity can exist with either representational imagery or abstract forms.

The forks in **B** vary quite humorously from delicate silverware to a garden pitchfork, and appear to be arranged to emphasize this contrast. The unity of the forms, based on a similar simple shape, would be apparent to us even if these were unfamiliar objects.

Seen simply as cut-out shapes, the variety of silhouettes in **C** would be apparent. Alex Katz balances this variation with the unity of the repeated portrait of his wife Ada. This approach of theme and variation is the essence of the concept of unity.

Unity of design is planned and controlled by an artist. Sometimes it stems naturally from the elements chosen, as in these examples. But more often it reflects the skill of the designer to create a unified pattern from varied elements. Another term for ''design'' is the word **composition,** which implies the same feeling of organization. Just as ''composition'' in a writing class is not merely a haphazard collection of words and punctuation marks, so a visual composition is not a careless scattering of random items around a format.

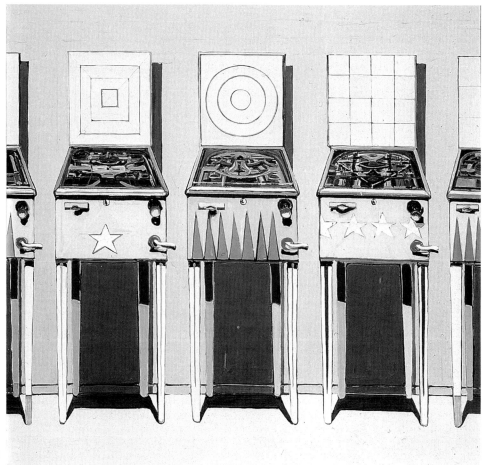

A

B

A Wayne Thiebaud. *Four Pinball Machines.* 1962. Oil on canvas, 67½ × 72″ (171 × 183 cm). Private collection, courtesy of the artist.

B Despite differences in appearance, all the objects have characteristics in common.

C Alex Katz. *Black Jacket.* 1972. Oil on aluminum (cutout), 62⅝ × 36¼″ (159 × 92 cm). Des Moines Art Center (gift in honor of Mrs. E. T. Meredith, Permanent Collection, 1978.7).

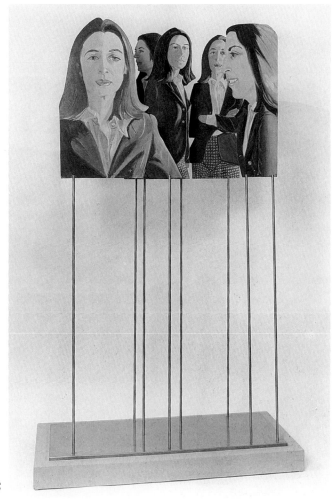

C

A Collage for *National Geographic* magazine. January
1988. Fred Otnes, Designer. © National Geographic
Society.
B There is an obvious visual similarity of elements.
C Poster for ''Out to Lunch'' concert series in
downtown Seattle. Designers: Pat Hansen, Jesse
Doquilo; Illustrator: Steve Coppin. © Hansen Design
Company, Seattle.

INTRODUCTION

An important aspect of visual unity is that the whole must be predominant over the parts: you must first see the *whole* pattern before you notice the individual elements. Each item may have a meaning and certainly add to the total effect, but the viewer must first see the pattern as a whole, rather than merely a collection of bits and pieces.

This concept differentiates a design from the usual scrapbook page. In a scrapbook each item is meant to be observed and studied individually, to be enjoyed and then forgotten as your eye moves on to the next souvenir. The result may be interesting but is not a unified design.

The **collage** in **A** is a design. It is similar to a scrapbook in that it contains many diverse elements, but we are aware first of the total pattern they make together and then we begin to enjoy the items separately.

Do not confuse *intellectual unity* with *visual unity*. **Visual unity** denotes some harmony or agreement between the items that is apparent to the *eye*. To say that a scrapbook page is unified because all the items have a common theme (your family, your wedding, your vacation at the beach) is unity of *idea*—that is, a conceptual unity not observable by the eye. A unifying *idea* will not necessarily produce a unified pattern.

The fact that all the elements in **A** deal with African-American History is interesting but irrelevant to the visual organization.

The unity in **B** does not derive from recognizing all the items in the design as bits of rope, string, thread, and so on. The visual unity stems from the repetition of linear, horizontal elements and the oval interruptions provided by the knots. Then the varying thicknesses and textures in an irregular spatial pattern add interest.

The need for visual unity does not deny that very often there is also an intellectual pleasure in design. Many times the task of a designer is to convey an idea or theme. Now the visual unity function is important along with an intellectual "reading" of the design. One example can show this dual appreciation. The poster in **C** is for a series of noontime concerts in downtown Seattle. The unity (and idea) is immediately seen in a design of lined-up lunch bags. Each bag contains an element of the varied programs. Then we realize the bag shapes themselves become like buildings on city blocks with tiny trees to express the "downtown" theme.

C

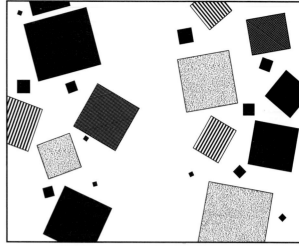

A

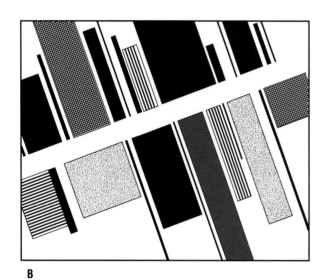

B

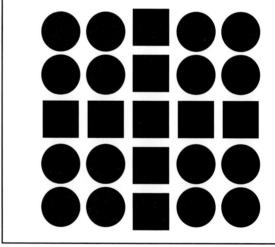

C

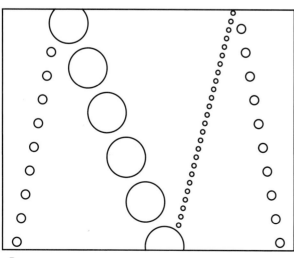

D

A   We instantly see two groups of shapes.
B   The white diagonal is as obvious as the two groups of rectangles.
C   Grouping similar shapes makes us see a plus sign in the center.
D   The circles seem to form ''lines,'' and we see an *M*-shape.
E   Piano & Rogers; Ove Arup & Partners. Centre National d'Art et de Culture George Pompidou (Beaubourg), Paris. 1971–77.

GESTALT

The designer's job in creating a visual unity is made easier by the fact that the viewer is actually *looking* for some sort of organization, something to relate the various elements. The viewer does not *want* to see confusion or unrelated chaos. The designer must provide some clues, but the viewer is already attempting to find some coherent pattern and unity. Indeed, when such a pattern cannot be found, it seems the viewer will turn away and simply ignore the image.

This is one of the conclusions that studies in the area of perception have shown. Since early in this century psychologists have done a great deal of research on visual perception, attempting to discover just how the eye and brain function together. Much of this research is, of course, very technical and scientific. The artist or designer can find it useful to understand some of the basic findings. The most widely known of these perception studies is called the **gestalt** theory of visual psychology.

Look at a few simple and elementary concepts that only begin to suggest the range of these studies and their conclusions:

The viewer tends to *group* objects that are close to each other into a larger unit. Therefore, our first impression of **A** is not merely some random squares but two groups of smaller elements.

Negative (or empty spaces) will likewise be organized. In **B** the many elements immediately are seen as two groups. However, with all the shapes ending on two common boundaries, the impression of the slanted white diagonal shape is as strong as the various rectangles.

Our brain will tend to relate and group objects of a similar shape. Hence, in **C** a cross or plus sign is obvious rather than an allover pattern of small shapes.

In **D** the pattern is not merely many circles of various sizes. Instead we will *close* the spaces between similar ones to form a design of ''lines.'' These diagonal ''lines'' organize themselves to give the impression of an *M* shape.

The list of examples could go on and on.

The Beaubourg **(E)** is a contemporary art center in Paris. It presents a complicated visual pattern by virtue of its ''inside-out'' appearance. Many of the conduits and structural features that are usually hidden form the outer shell of the building. This potentially chaotic assortment of pipes and scaffolding is given visual unity by the constant repetition of vertical ducts, square structural framing, and *X*-shaped supports. This building's distinct appearance stands in contrast to the other buildings of the area, further strengthening its visual identity. Our brain looks for similar elements, and when we recognize them we see a cohesive design rather than unorganized chaos.

E

WAYS TO ACHIEVE UNITY

PROXIMITY

An easy way to gain unity—to make separate elements look as if they belong together—is by **proximity,** simply putting the elements close together. The four elements in **A** appear isolated, as floating bits with no relationship to each other. By putting them close together **(B)**, we begin to see them as a total, related pattern. Proximity is a common unifying factor. Through proximity we recognize constellations in the skies and, in fact, are able to read. Change the proximity scheme that makes letters into words and reading becomes impossible.

The painting by Thomas P. Anshutz **(C)** of workers on their lunch break shows the idea in composition. The lighter elements of the workers' half-stripped bodies contrast with the generally darker background. However, these light elements are not placed aimlessly around the composition but, by proximity, are arranged carefully to unite visually. Arms stretch and reach out to touch or overlap adjoining figures so the bodies form a large horizontal unit stretching across the painting.

A. J. Alper's illustration **(D)** is an interesting collection of still-life objects that are grouped in clusters, such as a trio of mushrooms on the plate and a pair of bottles side by side. Notice how these small clusters connect, forming the larger constellation of the whole composition. The elements are visually tied together by proximity. Our eyes move smoothly from one item to the next.

Proximity is the simplest way to achieve unity, and many artworks employ this technique. Without proximity (with largely isolated elements), the artist must put greater stress on other methods to unify an image.

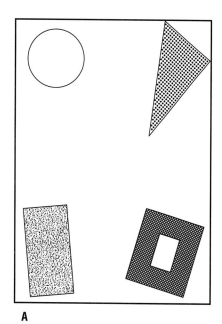

A

A If they are isolated from one another, elements appear unrelated.

B Placing items close together makes us see them first as a group.

C Thomas P. Anshutz. *The Ironworkers' Noontime.* 1880. Oil on canvas, 17 × 24″ (43.2 × 61 cm). The Fine Arts Museums of San Francisco (gift of Mr. and Mrs. John D. Rockefeller 3rd, 1979.7.4).

D A. J. Alper. *Champagne.* 1988. Oil on canvas, 22 × 28″ (56 × 71 cm). © A. J. Alper.

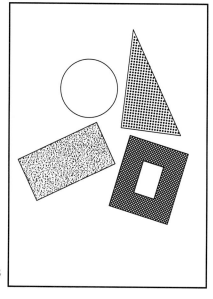

B

C

D

WAYS TO ACHIEVE UNITY

REPETITION

A valuable and widely used device for achieving visual unity is **repetition.** As the term implies, something simply repeats in various parts of the design to relate the parts to each other. The element that repeats may be almost anything—a color, a shape, a texture, a direction, or an angle. In the painting by Sophie Taeuber-Arp **(A)**, the composition is based on one shape: a circle with two circular "bites" removed. This shape is repeated in different sizes, directions, and positions. The result is a composition that is unified but not predictable.

Arman's sculpture **(B)** also shows unity by repetition. The obvious aspect is the repetition of the guitars, but we can also see a playful arrangement of shapes similar to Arp's. The guitars are presented in disassembled form. The parts are repeated in various positions, accentuating their shapes and revealing fresh aspects of a familiar subject. A composition, which might have been chaotic, is unified through repetition of shapes.

Similarly, in a representational painting repetition can be a unifying factor. In Degas' *The Millinery Shop* **(C)**, notice how often the artist repeats a circle motif. Just as in **A**, circles are a repeating element of visual unity, but now the circles represent objects such as hats, flowers, bows, the woman's head, bosom, and skirt, and so forth. The painting is a whole design of circles broken by a few verticals (the hat stand, the ribbons, the back draperies) and a triangle or two (the table, the woman's bent arm, and the front hat's ribbons). When we look beyond the subject matter in art, we begin to recognize the artist's use of repetition to create a sense of unity.

In paintings or designs with color, repetition can be an immediate way to create unity.

SEE ALSO: *Rhythm, pages 95 to 105.*

A

B

A Sophie Taeuber-Arp. *Composition with Circles Shaped by Curves.* 1935. Gouache on paper, 13⅞ × 10⅝″ (35 × 27 cm). Kunstmuseum Bern.

B Arman. *Á Ma Jolie.* 1982. Sliced bronze miniature guitars, 28 × 10¼ × 10¼″ (71 × 26 × 26 cm).

C Edgar Degas. *The Millinery Shop.* 1879–1884. Oil on canvas, 39⅛ × 43⅜″ (100 × 110.7 cm). Photograph courtesy The Art Institute of Chicago (Mr. and Mrs. Lewis Larned Coburn Memorial Collection, 1933.428).

C

A Proximity and similarity unify a design.

B The unity of the same elements is intensified when the elements are brought into contact with each other in a continuing line.

C Pablo Picasso. *La Joie de Vivre or Antipolis.* 1946. Painting on fiber reinforced cement. 47¼ × 98½″ (1.2 × 2.5 m). Picasso Museum, Antibes, France.

D Edgar Degas, *The Tub.* 1886. Pastel, 23½ × 32⅓″ (60 × 82 cm). Musée d'Orsay, Paris.

E Jan Groover. *Untitled.* 1987. Gelatin-silver print, 11¹⁵⁄₁₆ × 14¹⁵⁄₁₆″ (30 × 38 cm). Robert Miller Gallery, New York.

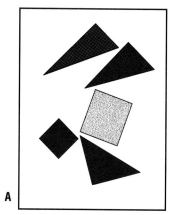

A

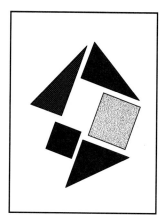

B

C

D

WAYS TO ACHIEVE UNITY

CONTINUATION

A third way to achieve unity is by **continuation,** a more subtle device than proximity or repetition, which are fairly obvious. Continuation, naturally, means that something ''continues''— usually a line, an edge, or a direction from one form to another. The viewer's eye is carried smoothly from one to the next.

The design in **A** is unified by the closeness and the character of the elements. In **B** though, the shapes seem even more of a unit, since they are arranged in such a way that one's vision flows easily from one element to the next. The shapes no longer float casually. They are now organized into a definite, set pattern.

Human figures, animals, plants, and a ship are drawn in whimsical abstract form in Picasso's painting **(C)**. Notice how the majority of these shapes share an edge with two strong, wavy, horizontal lines extending across the canvas. This continuation visually unites the forms.

The pastel drawing by Degas **(D)** is much more naturalistic, with the forms quite representational. But the same use of continuation can be seen as the eye is carried from one form to another by placement. The line of the round tub starts at the bather's hairline, meets her fingertips, and joins the vertical line of the shelf where the brush handle overlaps. The circular shape of the bather's hips is tangential to the same shelf edge. Notice the careful arrangement of the objects on the shelf— how each item barely touches or carries the eye to another. That at first glance the arrangement seemed casual and unplanned only adds to our admiration of the artist.

A deliberate or more obvious form of continuation is a striking aspect in many of Jan Groover's photographs. In one series of photographs she would catch passing trucks as an edge of the truck would visually align with a distant roof line or a foreground pole. This alignment would connect these disparate elements for an instant, resulting in a unified image. In **E** Groover employs a more subtle form of continuation, which results in a fluid eye movement around the picture. One shape leads to the next, and coincidental alignments are part of this flow.

E

WAYS TO ACHIEVE UNITY

CONTINUITY

Continuation is the planned arrangement of various forms so that their edges are lined up—hence forms that are ''continuous'' from one to another within a design.

When the artist is creating a single design, the choices are almost unlimited in how the concept of continuation can be applied. The task changes, however, when there are multiple units. The job now is not only to unify one design, but to create several designs that somehow seem to relate to each other. In other words, all the designs seem part of a ''series''—the same unifying theme continues in successive designs. This is not an unusual job for a designer. Countless books, catalogs, magazines, pamphlets, and so on, all require this designing skill.

The term often used is **continuity.** This denotes there is now a visual relationship between two or more individual designs. An aid often used in such serial designs is the **grid.**

The artist begins by designing a grid, a network of horizontal and vertical intersecting lines that divide the page and create a framework of areas such as **A.** Then this same ''skeleton'' is used on all succeeding pages for a consistency of spacing and design results throughout all the units. To divide any format into areas or modules permits, of course, innumerable possibilities, so there is no predetermined pattern or solution. In creating the original grid, there are often numerous technical considerations that would determine the solution. But the basic idea is easily understood.

Using the same grid (or space division) on each successive page might suggest that a sameness, and hence boring regularity, would result from repetition. This, however, is not true. A great deal of variety is possible within any framework, as the varied page layouts in **B** and **C** show.

As the computer becomes more and more important in graphic design, techniques such as the grid will become very common.

Sometimes the same grid will be used on all publications by a company so they all share a visual unity and what is called a ''corporate identity.'' We are all familiar with examples of this. Sometimes a company, over a period of weeks or months, runs a series of advertisements that have an identical layout. The illustrations and copy change, but the basic space division stays the same. Often a single glimpse of the page identifies the advertiser in our minds because we are already so familiar with the overall format.

A A grid determines page margins and divides the format into areas used on successive layouts.

B A grid need not lead to a boring regularity in page design.

C Wide variety is possible within the basic framework.

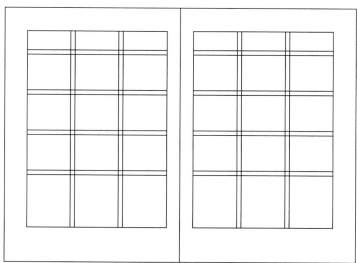

A

ARCHITECTURE

B

MUSIC

C

UNITY WITH VARIETY

The word *design* implies the idea that the various components of a visual image are organized into a cohesive pattern. A design must have visual unity.

The checkerboard pattern in **A** has complete unity. It is very easy for us to see the constant repetition of shape and the obvious continuation of lined-up edges. Unhappily, the result is also quite boring. In the design in **B** there is the same repetitive division of space, but it doesn't seem quite as dull. There are now some changes (or variations) that make this design a bit more interesting to the eye. In **C** the variations have been enlarged so we can almost forget the dull checkerboard in **A**. But the same underlying elements of unity are still present. This is the basis of the principle **unity with variety.** There is an obvious, underlying feeling of unity, yet variations enliven the pattern. Shapes may repeat, but perhaps in different sizes; colors may repeat, but perhaps in different values.

The nineteenth-century American quilt in **D** is obviously a basic checkerboard design, as are many quilts due to the method of construction. While the same square shapes repeat over and over, there is a fantastic variety of small designs—no two exactly alike.

In the collage by Rauschenberg (**E**) an underlying feeling of a checkerboard is again the basic space division. The feeling now is more casual and fluid. In an irregular way, the elements vary in size and color. There is not the rigid lining up of edges seen in **A**. Our first attention is directed to the contrasting variety of historical art images. But the basic planned structure is also clear and provides a framework.

A point to remember is that, with a great variety of elements, a simple layout idea can give needed unity and be very effective.

A

B

C

D

A checkerboard shows perfect unity.

Some variations in the basic pattern increase interest.

More variation possibilities are endless.

Quilt. Ca. 1885. Silk and velvet, 79 × 67″ (2 × 1.7 m). America Hurrah Antiques, New York.

Robert Rauschenberg. *Centennial Certificate.* 1969. Color lithograph, 35⅞ × 25″ (91 × 64 cm). The Metropolitan Museum of Art, New York (Florence and Joseph Singer Collection, 1969.630).

A
B
C
D
E

E

A

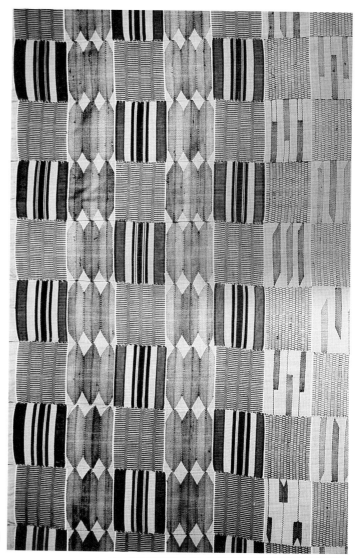

A Barbara Hepworth. *Maquette, Theme and Variations.*
1970. Bronze, 11⅜ × 16⅛″ (29 × 41 cm). Private
collection, courtesy Hepworth Estate, St. Ives,
Cornwall, U.K.
B West African Kente cloth. No date. Cotton, 82¼ ×
132½″ (2 × 3.5 m). Anacostia Museum, Smithsonian
Institution, Washington, DC.
C Valerie Clarke. *The Waiting Room.* 1984. Thirteen
photographic panels, 25″ × 15′ (64 cm × 4.6 m).
Installation, The Women's Center, University of
Michigan–Flint.

B

UNITY WITH VARIETY

Is the principle of **unity with variety** a conscious, planned ingredient supplied by the artist or designer, or is it something that a confident designer produces automatically? There is no real answer. The only certainty is that the principle can be seen in art from every different period, culture, and geographic area.

The relief sculpture in **A** is titled *Maquette, Theme and Variations*. The decision to create a composition of three panels unified by the constant repetition of half circles as a ''theme'' was clearly an initial and deliberate choice of the artist. The many changes in size and position of these bronze forms on each panel then provide the ''variations'' of the title.

The use of unity with variety displayed by the woven fabric from West Africa **(B)** suggests a more intuitive approach. Since many designs employ traditional motifs, the method was undoubtedly ''learned,'' but not at an art school or from a textbook. Yet the design illustrates the principle clearly. The basic pattern is a very simple dark-and-light checkerboard with a

vertical emphasis, as most areas stress vertical geometric patterns. Textures and light-and-dark designs vary in an irregular way using very simple elements. The idea of related variations seems to provide a basic satisfaction that can be arrived at without theoretical discussions of aesthetics.

A conscious (or obvious) use of unity with variety does not necessarily lessen our pleasure as viewers. A very obvious use of the principle is not a drawback. Valerie Clarke's work in **C** immediately shows unity. Thirteen photographs of the same size are rigidly lined up. The background white wall repeats, and the line of the bench continues from one photograph to another. We then concentrate on the various poses of the women artists and the surprise of one empty frame. This obvious use of unity with variety was certainly carefully planned. But the result puts the emphasis where it was intended: on the figures.

C

UNITY WITH VARIETY

EMPHASIS ON UNITY

In the application of any art principle, wide flexibility is possible within the general framework of the guideline. So it is with the idea of **unity with variety.** To say a design must contain both the ordered quality of unity and the lively quality of variety does not limit or inhibit the artist. The principle can encompass a wide variety of extremely different visual images.

These pages show successful examples in which the unifying element of repetition is emphasized. Variety is present, but admittedly in a subtle, understated way. The Diane Arbus photograph shown in **A** intrigues us in the same way we are fascinated in life when we meet ''identical'' twins. Such perfect repetition is unexpected, so we proceed to search for the tiny differences and variety we know exists in nature and, hence, in art.

We know at a glance that all the plants depicted in **B** are irises. As with other Japanese screens from this period, the composition is strongly unified by repetition of natural forms. But this is *not* wallpaper. No two leaves or flowers are identical, and the eye is rewarded with subtle variations on a constant theme.

The visual unity gained by repetition is immediately apparent, in fact, almost overwhelmingly so, in **C**, an example of **minimalism.** Artists such as Don Judd seek to reduce art to a minimum of aesthetic considerations. To focus our attention on the real, physical presence of his simple forms, compositional variations are purposely de-emphasized. The rigidly concentric alignment of boxes provides no apparent shape contrast or placement variation. Our attention must be directed to how any change in this sculpture will come only through the viewer's change of position or vantage point. Such artworks have sometimes been criticized as ''too dull'' or ''too cold and sterile.'' Many of these comments are by people who have never read or heard of the phrase ''unity with variety.'' Nevertheless, they are using the basic concept in their criticism. What these comments truly mean is that the design has an overwhelming unity, but the variety is so subtle as to be insufficient for the particular viewer's taste. The ''correct'' balance between unity and variety—between control and spontaneous freedom—varies with the individual artist, with the theme or purpose, and eventually with the viewer.

A

B

A Diane Arbus. *Identical twins, Roselle, N.J., 1967.* 1967. Photograph. Copyright © Estate of Diane Arbus 197l; photo courtesy Robert Miller Gallery, New York.

B Ogata Kōrin. *Irises.* Edo Period, ca. 1705. Six-fold screen, color on gold foil over paper, 5′ × 11′2″ (150.9 × 338.8 cm). Nezu Institute of Fine Arts, Tokyo.

C Donald Judd. *Untitled.* 1992. Purple plexiglas and stainless steel, 10 units, each 6⅛ × 27 × 24″ (15.2 × 68.5 × 61 cm); overall, installed 10' × 27″ × 24″ (304.8 × 68.5 × 61 cm). Photograph courtesy The Pace Gallery, New York.

C

UNITY WITH VARIETY

EMPHASIS ON VARIETY

Life is not always orderly and rational. Often life brings surprises, the unexpected, and experiences that seem chaotic and hectic. To express this aspect of life, many artists have purposely chosen to underplay the unifying components of their work and let the elements appear at least superficially uncontrolled and free of any formal design restraints. The examples here show works in which the element of **variety** is paramount.

The immediate impression of the *Print* magazine cover in **A** is one of a haphazard conglomeration of incongruous images. Only the fact that they're close together seems to give any sort of unity. This design, by computer artist John Hersey, represents the disjointed, fragmented, eccentric images we see each day (and take for granted) on our television screens and in our newspapers.

The California house in **B** is unusual, as so often architecture is rather formal and regular in design. Here, just when we think we find an orderly pattern, some elements disrupt it. The result is surprising and intriguing. ''Playful'' is a term often applied to such a design, and it should not be interpreted as a disparaging adjective. ''Play'' by nature is fun, casual, and unexpected. Within limits, it's a legitimate goal of art.

Complicated, twisting linear forms dominate the Pollock painting in **C**. There is no subject matter except for the idea of dynamics and change. A feeling of unplanned, totally spontaneous movement pervades the image. In galleries or museums, when expressionist abstractions such as **C** are exhibited, one constantly overhears such criticisms as ''I don't like it—too messy,'' ''too wild and uncontrolled,'' and even ''my two-year-old could do *that.*'' What these self-styled critics are saying is that the variety in such a picture is extremely obvious, but their eyes cannot discern any sense of order or unity imposed on that variety. The scales have tipped too far in one direction for them.

Without some aspect of unity, an image becomes chaotic and quickly ''unreadable.'' Without some elements of variety, an image is lifeless and dull and becomes uninteresting. Neither utter confusion nor utter regularity are visually desirable. Beyond this general guideline the options of the artist are very broad.

A John Hersey. Cover design for *Print* magazine. March/April 1992. © John Hersey 1992.
B Frank Gehry. *Norton Beach House.* Venice, CA. 1984. Photo: © Michael Moran.
C Jackson Pollock. *Echo (Number 25, 1951).* 1951. Enamel on unprimed canvas, 91⅞ × 86″ (233.3 × 218.4 cm). Collection, The Museum of Modern Art, New York (acquired through the Lillie P. Bliss Bequest).

A

B

C

3

EMPHASIS

FOCAL POINT

INTRODUCTION

There are very few artists or designers who do not want people to look at their work. In past centuries, when pictures were rare, almost any image was guaranteed attention. Today, with photography and an abundance of books, magazines, newspapers, signs, and so on, all of us are confronted daily with hundreds of pictures. We take this abundance for granted, but it makes the artist's job more difficult. Without an audience's attention, any message, any artistic or aesthetic values, are lost.

How does a designer catch a viewer's attention? How does the artist provide a pattern that attracts the eye? Nothing will guarantee success, but one device that can help is a point of emphasis or **focal point.** This emphasized element initially can attract attention and encourage the viewer to look further.

It is almost impossible to look at **A** and not first notice the nude lady at the left. The painting has many elements: lions, jungle flowers and trees, a native, even an elephant, but our eye is first of all drawn to the lady. This is the concept of a focal point.

Even in purely abstract or nonobjective patterns, a focal point will attract the viewer's eye and give some contrast and visual emphasis. The painting by Stuart Davis **(B)** is a pattern of simple, bold forms in bright, flat colors. The more complicated curving black shape near the center provides a change and becomes the focal point.

The poster in **C** is a very complicated and diverse pattern, as befits a major international exhibition of art. However, the checkerboard is an obvious focal point in a very complicated design. Then we begin to notice the repetition of shapes, horizontals, and so on, that give visual unity.

There can be more than one focal point. Sometimes secondary points of emphasis are present that have less attention value than the focal point. These are called **accents.**

However, the designer must be careful. Several focal points of equal emphasis can turn the design into a three-ring circus in which the viewer does not know where to look first. Interest is replaced by confusion: when *everything* is emphasized, *nothing* is emphasized.

A

B

A Henri Rousseau. *The Dream*. 1910. Oil on canvas, 6′ 8½″ × 9′9½″ (204.5 × 298.5 cm). The Museum of Modern Art, New York (gift of Nelson A. Rockefeller).

B Stuart Davis. *Ready to Wear*. 1955. Oil on canvas, 56 × 42″ (142.9 × 106.7 cm). Photograph courtesy of The Art Institute of Chicago (gift of Mr. and Mrs. Sigmund Kunstadter and Goodman Fund, 1956.137).

C Rico Lins. Poster for the XXI International Biennial, São Paulo, Brazil. 1991. Design © Rico Lins 1991.

C

WAYS TO ACHIEVE EMPHASIS

EMPHASIS BY CONTRAST

Very often in art the pictorial emphasis is clear, and in simple compositions (such as a portrait) the focal point is obvious. But the more complicated the pattern, the more necessary or helpful a focal point may become in organizing the design.

As a general rule, a focal point results when one element differs from the others. Whatever interrupts an overall feeling or pattern automatically attracts the eye by this difference. The possibilities are almost endless:

When most of the elements are dark, a light form breaks the pattern and becomes a focal point.

When almost all the elements (whether light or dark) are vertical, a diagonal element is emphasized **(A)**.

In an overall design of distorted expressionistic forms, the sudden introduction of a naturalistic image **(B)** will draw the eye for its very different style.

When many elements are about the same size, similar but unexpectedly smaller ones become visually important **(C)**.

When the majority of shapes are rectilinear and angular parallelograms, round shapes stand out **(D)**.

This list could go on and on; many other possibilities will occur to you. Sometimes this idea is called **emphasis by contrast.** The element that contrasts with, rather than continues, the prevailing design scheme becomes the focal point.

Color is an element often used to achieve emphasis by contrast. A change in color or a change in brightness can immediately attract our attention.

SEE ALSO: *Devices to Show Depth/Size, pages 168–170, Value as Emphasis, page 216, and Color as Emphasis, page 238.*

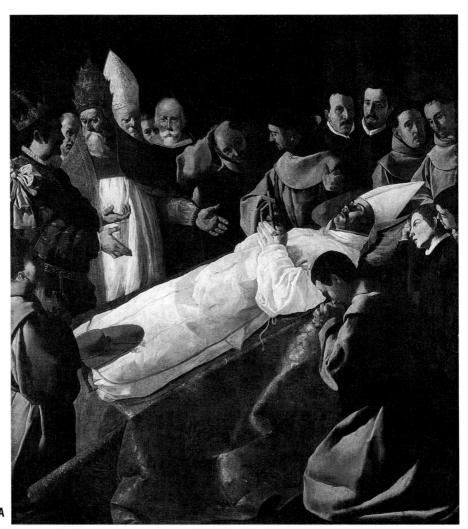

A

B

A Francisco Zurbarán. *The Funeral of Saint Bonaventure*. 1629. Oil on canvas, 8'2" × 7'4" (250 × 225 cm). Musée du Louvre, Paris.
B James Ensor. *Portrait of the Artist Surrounded by Masks*. 1889. Oil, 47½ × 31½" (121 × 80 cm).
C Fernando Botero. *Night in Colombia.* 1980. Oil on canvas, 74 × 91" (188 × 231.1 cm). Metropolitan Museum of Art, New York (anonymous gift, 1983.251).
D László Moholy-Nagy. *A II*. 1924. Oil on canvas, 3'9⅝" × 4'5⅝" (l.16 × 1.36 m). Solomon R. Guggenheim Museum, New York.

C

D

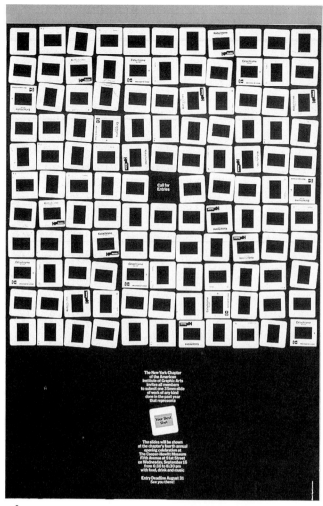

A Call for entries for AIGA/New York show, ''Take Your Best Shot''. Designer: Michael Beirut, Vignelli Associates, New York.
B Paul Cézanne. *Still Life with Apples and Peaches.* Ca. 1905. Oil on canvas, 32 × 39⅝″ (81 × 100 cm). © 1993 National Gallery of Art, Washington, D.C. (gift of Eugene and Agnes E. Meyer).
C Edwin Romanzo Elmer. *Mourning Picture.* 1890. Oil on canvas, 28 × 36″ (71 × 92 cm). Smith College Museum of Art (purchase).

A

B

WAYS TO ACHIEVE EMPHASIS

EMPHASIS BY ISOLATION

A variation on the device of emphasis by contrast is the useful technique of **emphasis by isolation.** There is no way we can look at the design in **A** and not focus our attention on that element at the bottom. It is absolutely identical with all the elements above. But simply by being alone, by itself, it gets our attention. This is contrast, of course, but it is contrast of placement, not form. In such a case, the element, as here, need not be any different from the others.

In the still life by Cézanne (**B**) the pitcher at left repeats the color of the bowl and the cloth, and the design on it repeats the fruit forms. In short, the pitcher is part of a unified composition, but it gains visual importance because it sits away from the items grouped together at right. The pitcher is an emphasized element only through its detached position.

Mourning Picture (**C**) is a rather haunting painting as it commemorates the death of the artist's young daughter. In this nineteenth-century work, the young girl is the obvious focal point. It is not merely that she is the largest element. She is isolated on the left-hand side with her head carefully silhouetted against the light sky. The house and other figures are grouped together on the right. Her separation seems to be not only an emphasis but also an emotional aspect of the work.

In neither of these examples is the focal point directly in the center of the composition. This placement could appear *too* obvious and contrived. However, it is wise to remember that a focal point placed too close to an edge will have a tendency to pull the viewer's eye right out of the picture. Notice in the Cézanne still life (**B**) how the verticals of the drapery on the left side keep the isolated pitcher from directing our gaze out of the picture. In **C** the girl's look to the right and the white lamb and the doll carriage tie the two sides of the painting together.

C

A Our eyes are drawn to the central element of this design by all the elements radiating from it.

B John Steuart Curry. *Baptism in Kansas*. 1928. Oil on canvas, 3′4″ × 4′2″ (1.02 × 1.27 m). Whitney Museum of American Art, New York (gift of Gertrude Vanderbilt Whitney, 31.159).

C Maurice Utrillo. *Church of Le Sacré Coeur, Montmartre et rue Saint-Rustique*. N.d. Oil on canvas, 19⅝ × 24″ (50 × 61 cm). Courtesy, Museum of Fine Arts, Boston (bequest of John T. Spaulding).

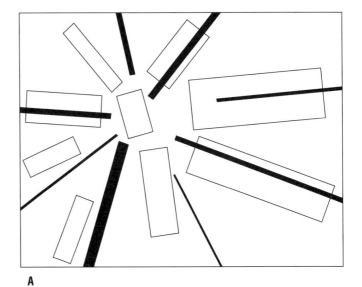

A

B

WAYS TO ACHIEVE EMPHASIS

EMPHASIS BY PLACEMENT

The placement of elements in a design may function in another way to create emphasis. If many elements point to one item, our attention is directed there, and a focal point results. A **radial** design is a perfect example of this device. Just as all forms radiate from the convergent focus, so they also repeatedly lead our eyes back to this central element. As **A** illustrates, this central element may be like other forms in the design; the emphasis results from the placement, not from any difference in character of the form itself.

Radial designs are more common in architecture or the craft areas than in two-dimensional art. The more subtle variation in painting occurs when many figures *look* (or sometimes point) in a common direction. In life when we see someone staring or pointing in a certain way, we have an almost uncontrollable urge to look there. This happens in art, too. In Curry's

scene of a fundamentalist baptism by immersion **(B)**, all the figures look directly at the preacher and the girl, automatically directing our eyes there as well. Even the lines of the windmill and the roofs of the barn and house direct our eyes to the focal point of these two figures.

In Utrillo's painting **(C)** the domed church is the focal point, though it is small and ''farthest'' away from us. But, just as in the design in **A**, all the other larger elements point our eyes towards it. The perspective lines of buildings, roofs, fence, and the street all direct our eyes back to the church.

The effect need not be as obvious as in these examples. However, once your focal point has been decided upon, it is wise to avoid having other major or visually important elements point or lead the eye *away* from it. Confusion of emphasis can result.

C

A

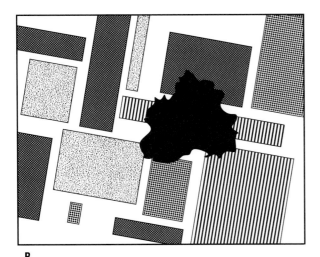

B

C

DEGREE OF EMPHASIS

A specific theme may, at times, call for a dominant, even visually overwhelming focal point. The use of a strong visual emphasis on one element is not unusual.

In the graphic design of newspaper advertisements, billboards, magazine covers, and so on, we often see an obvious emphasis on one element. This can be necessary to attract the viewer's eye and present the theme (or product) in the few seconds most people look casually at such material. The very large scale *X* in **A** is also a bright orange against the black-and-white background photograph. It is an immediate focal point, attracts our attention to the page, and also conveys immediately an idea of the theme of the article.

A focal point, however strong, should remain related to and a part of the overall design. The *X* in **A** is dominating visually, yet is related to other elements in placement and character. Contrast the effect in **A** with that in **B**. In **B** the focal point is obvious again. But here the large, irregular black shape is very different from the subtle rectangular shapes forming the rest of the design. Somehow it seems *too* strong and rather to overwhelm the rest of the pattern. To a lesser extent the same criticism might apply to the painting by Bonnard **(C)**. The isolated, black, oval tray in the center foreground is clearly a focal point. But again it seems too dominant; this sudden dark spot seems out of keeping with the subtle value and color changes in the rest of the painting.

In general, the principle of unity and the creation of a harmonious pattern with related elements is more important than the injection of a focal point if this point would jeopardize the design's unity. In Juan Gris' still life **(D)**, the massed group of linear circles defining the bunch of grapes is a focal point. But the values of this element are repeated in several other places. And circular forms are seen elsewhere, with the bottle top and glass bottom repeating the same small linear circle motif. The focal point established is not a completely unrelated element.

A Cover of *Seattle Weekly* newspaper. November 18, 1992. Designer: Fred Andrews, Sasquatch Publishing Co.; Photographer: David Lee, Warner Bros. Courtesy Sasquatch Publishing Co.

B The black shape seems too strong and unrelated to other elements.

C Pierre Bonnard. *Coffee*. Ca. 1914. Oil on canvas, 28¾ × 41⅞″ (73 × 106.4 cm). Tate Gallery, London. Reproduced by courtesy of the Trustees.

D Juan Gris. *Bottle, Glass and Fruit Dish*. 1921. Oil on canvas, 24 × 20″ (61 × 50 cm). Kunstmuseum Basel (Emmanuel Hoffman Foundation).

D

ABSENCE OF FOCAL POINT

A definite focal point is not a necessity in creating a successful design. It is a tool that artists may or may not use, depending on their aims. An artist may wish to emphasize the entire surface of a composition over any individual elements. Lee Krasner's painting **(A)** is an example. Similar shapes and textures are repeated throughout the painting. The artist creates an ambiguous visual environment that is puzzling. Dark and light areas repeat over the surface in an even distribution, and no one area stands out. The painting has no real starting point or visual climax.

Sometimes the artist's theme might suggest the absence of a focal point. In Andy Warhol's painting **(B)** there are a hundred repetitions of precisely the same image with no change, no contrast, and no point of emphasis. But the repetitive, unrelieved quality is the basic point and dictated the design. The painting contains a serious comment on our taken-for-granted daily lives. The design reflects life today, where we are bombarded with insistent and strident repetition of the same commercial images over and over.

Some art forms by their very nature rule out the use of a focal point. Woven and printed fabrics generally have no focal point but consist of an unstressed repetition of a motif over the whole surface. A focal point on draperies, bedspreads, or upholstery might be distracting. In clothing the focal point is provided by the design of the garment.

Since a focal point is such a common artistic device, sometimes attention can be gotten by simply *not* using one. There is no dominant element in the poster in **C**. Instead, we are intrigued by the pattern of widely different items, all with equal emphasis. The designer has achieved his goal: Our eye is attracted by the unusual overall emphasis of the layout, and we spend time studying the image.

SEE ALSO: *Crystallographic Balance, page 92.*

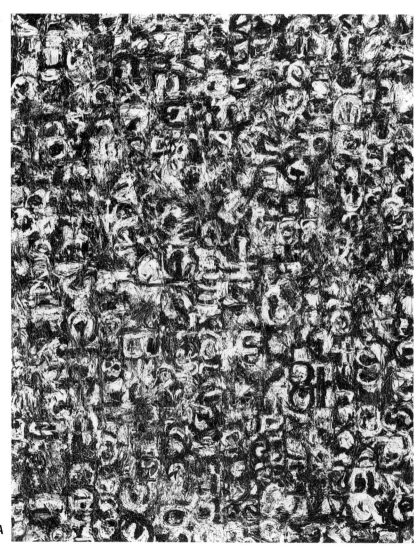

A

B

A Lee Krasner. *Untitled.* 1949. Oil on composition
  board, 48 × 37″ (122 × 94 cm). The Museum of
  Modern Art, New York (gift of Alfonso A. Ossorio).
B Andy Warhol. *100 Cans.* 1962. Oil on canvas, 6′ ×
  4′4″ (1.83 × 1.32 m). Albright-Knox Art Gallery,
  Buffalo, NY (gift of Seymour H. Knox, 1963).
C *Seasons Greetings from WGBH Design.* Poster. 1985.
  37 × 32″ (94 × 81.3 cm). Chris Pullman, Art
  Director; Gaye Korbet and Chris Pullman, Designers.
  Courtesy of WGBH Boston.

C

4

SCALE
PROPORTION

INTRODUCTION

Scale and *proportion* are related terms in that both refer basically to size. **Scale** is essentially another word for size. ''Large scale'' is a way of saying big, and ''small scale'' means small. ''Big'' and ''small,'' however, are relative. What is big? Big is meaningless unless we have some standard of reference. A big dog means nothing if we do not know the size of most dogs. This is what separates the two terms. **Proportion** refers to *relative* size, size measured against other elements or against some mental norm or standard.

The small stool and the clues provided by the architecture of the space provide a scale reference for judging the size of the sphere in **A**. Since a sphere has no inherent scale reference, we are dependent on the context to judge its size. In **A** the sphere is almost oppressively large in proportion to the setting. Imagine the same sphere outdoors seen from a high altitude in an airplane. It might have the same visual impact as a period on this page.

We often think of the word proportion in connection with mathematical systems of numerical ratios. It is true that historically many such systems have been developed. Artists have attempted to define the most pleasing size relationships in items as diverse as the width and length of sides of a rectangle to parts of the human body.

Scale and proportion are closely tied to emphasis and focal point. Large scale and especially large scale in proportion to other elements make for an obvious visual emphasis. In **B** the eye goes naturally first to the large-scale figure in the center. The artist Honoré Sharrer has created a focal point that dominates the other smaller figures in the windows of the building in the background.

In past centuries visual scale was often related to thematic importance. The size of figures was based on their symbolic importance in the subject being presented. In the tenth-century illumination **(C)**, the emperor on his throne has been drawn unnaturally large compared to the other figures. The artist thus immediately established not only an obvious focal point but indicated relative conceptual status of the ruler and his subjects. This use of scale is called **hieratic scaling.**

SEE ALSO: *Devices to Show Depth/Size, pages 168–170.*

A

B

A Richard Roth. *Untitled*. 1983. Installation: 11′
diameter (3.4 m) sphere with red stool. © 1993
Richard Roth.

B Honoré Sharrer. *The Industrial Scene*. Center panel
of *Tribute to the American Working People*. 1945–
1950. Oil on canvas, 25 × 31″ (63 × 79 cm).
National Museum of American Art.

C Emperor Otto II from the *Registrum Gregorii*. Trier,
Ca. 985. Manuscript illumination, 10⅝ × 7⅞″
(27 × 20 cm). Musée Condé, Chantilly.

C

A

A Nicholas Hilliard. *Self Portrait*. 1577. Diameter: 1⅝″ (4 cm). © The Board of Trustees of the Victoria & Albert Museum, London.

B Limbourg Brothers. *Multiplication of the Loaves and Fishes*, from the Book of Hours *(Les Très Riches Heures)* of the Duke of Berry. 1416. Manuscript illumination, 6¼ × 4⅜″ (16 × 11 cm). Musée Condé, Chantilly.

C Japanese Netsuke (detail). 18th century. Ivory, with lacquer inro and silver ojime. Height 2″ (5.1 cm). Metropolitan Museum of Art, New York (bequest of Mrs. H. O. Havemeyer, 1929, The H. O. Havemeyer Collection, 29.100.756).

D Kent Twitchell, *Ed Ruscha Monument*. 1987. Mural installation in Los Angeles, figure 70′ (21 m) high.

B

C

SCALE OF ART

One way to think of artistic scale is to consider the scale of the work itself—its size in relation to other art, in relation to its surroundings, or in relation to human size. Unhappily, the one thing book illustrations cannot do is show art in its original size or scale. Unusual or unexpected scale is arresting and attention-getting. Sheer size *does* impress us.

When we are confronted by frescoes such as the Sistine Chapel ceiling, our first reaction is simply awe at the enormous scope of the work. Later we study and admire details, but first we are overwhelmed by the sheer magnitude. The reverse effect is illustrated in **A**. It comes as a shock to realize that this portrait is a mere 1⅝ inches in diameter. The exquisite detail, the delicate precision at this scale is impressive. Our first thought has to be of the fantastic difficulty of achieving this in so tiny a format.

If large or small size springs naturally from the function, theme, or purpose of a work, an unusual scale is justified. We are acquainted with many such cases. The gigantic pyramids made a political statement of the Pharaoh's eternal power. The elegant miniatures of the religious book of hours **(B)** served as book illustrations for the private devotionals of medieval nobility. The Japanese sculpture in **C** is only 2 inches tall—smaller than you see it in the picture. This tiny piece of ivory carving had a utilitarian purpose. Called a *netsuke*, the piece was a small toggle (or clip) that secured pouches and other items hung from the Japanese *obi*, or waist sash. In this intricately detailed example a scholar rides through waves on a horned carp with tiny, black, coral-inlaid eyes.

The scale of **D** is the opposite approach. The scale of Kent Twitchell's enormous 70-foot-high wall painting dwarfs even today's large billboards. The cars photographed in the foreground give a feeling of the work's tremendous size. Naturalistic images blown up to such monumental scale cannot be ignored, and they alter the urban environment.

D

A

A Corson Hirschfeld. *Serpent Mound, Ohio*. 1982.
Painted black-and-white photograph. © Corson
Hirschfeld 1982.

B Claes Oldenburg. *Giant Three-Way Plug*. 1970.
Cor-ten steel and polished bronze, 60⅞ × 120⅝ ×
78″ (1.5 × 3 × 2 m). Allen Memorial Art Museum,
Oberlin College, Ohio (gift of the artist and Fund for
Contemporary Art, 1970).

C Edward Ruscha. *Actual Size*. 1962. Oil on canvas,
72 × 67″ (182.9 × 170.2 cm). The Los Angeles
County Museum of Art (anonymous gift through the
Contemporary Art Council).

B

SCALE OF ART

Earthworks are unique in the grandeur of their scale. The *Serpent Mound* **(A)** was created by Native Americans over two thousand years ago. Its original function or meaning has been lost, and is the subject of speculation. With a length of more than 1,300 feet, it is best experienced on foot. Only then can we relate the size of the mound to our own scale, and the landscape setting. The egg-shaped mound at the serpent's mouth is 158 feet long: this single element would be considered large in scale relative to our body as a reference.

Claes Oldenburg has made use of a leap of scale in his *Giant Three-Way Plug* **(B)**. As with the work of other pop artists, this piece calls attention to an everyday object, not previously considered worthy of aesthetic consideration. Oldenburg transforms the object by elevating it to a monumental scale. A magnification such as this allows us to see the form with fresh eyes, and as a result we might discover new associations, such as the male and female aspects of the form. It can also be argued that Oldenburg makes monuments appropriate to a consumer culture.

Unusual scale in a work of art should have a thematic or functional justification. The painting in **C** measures 5 feet by 6 feet. This is quite large for a painting, and with its few elements and very simple spatial pattern, the large size might seem misguided. However, *Actual Size* is described by the artist, Edward Ruscha, as a "commercial landscape." Thus the painting is a satire that is meant to mock the large scale and often inane content of the huge, strident billboards that demand our attention each day. The large lettering is "actual size" for a billboard, while the smaller depiction of the Spam can is also "actual size." The work's scale is an intrinsic part of the theme.

Here again the idea of proportion can be relevant. Works of art are often selected (or created) for specific locations, and their size in proportion to the setting is a prime consideration. A small religious painting appropriate in scale for a side chapel could be visually lost on the altar of a vast cathedral.

C

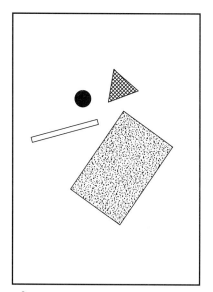
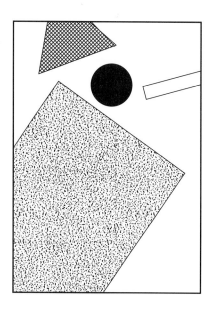
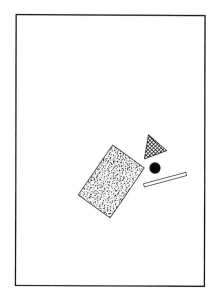

A Changes in scale within a design also change the total effect.

B Domenico Ghirlandaio. *The Last Supper*. Ca. 1480. Fresco, 25′7″ (8 m) wide. San Marco, Florence.

C Emil Nolde. *The Last Supper*. 1909. Oil on canvas, 34⅝ × 42½″ (88 × 108 cm). Statens Museum for Kunst, Copenhagen.

B

SCALE WITHIN ART

The second way to discuss artistic scale is to consider the size and scale of elements *within* the design or pattern. The scale here, of course, is relative to the overall area of the format; a big element in one painting might be small in a larger work. Again we often use the term **proportion** to describe the size relationships between various parts of a unit. To say an element in a composition is "out of proportion" carries a negative feeling. And it is true that such a visual effect is often startling or unsettling. However, it is possible that this reaction is precisely what some artists desire.

The three examples in **A** contain the same elements. But in each design the scale of the items is different, thus altering the proportional relationships between the parts. This variation results in very different visual effects, in the same way that altering the proportions of ingredients in a recipe changes the final dish. Which design is "best" or which we prefer can be argued. The answer would depend on what effect we wish to create.

Look at the differences scale can make in a painting. Examples **B** and **C** both deal with the same topic: the well-known story of Christ's Last Supper with His disciples before the crucifixion. In the painting by Ghirlandaio **(B)** all the figures are quite small. They are placed within a large, airy, and open space. The regular placement of the figures at the table and the geometric, repeating elements of the architecture give a feeling of calm and quiet order. *Last Supper* by Nolde **(C)** is, indeed, in a different style of painting, but a major difference in the two works is the use of scale within the picture. Nolde's figures are large-scale, crammed together in a constricting space. The result is crowded and claustrophobic. Nolde focuses our attention on the agony and suffering of the event. The harsh drawing, agitated brushwork, and distortion of the figures enforce the feeling. Both artists related the same story, but with very different goals. The choice of scale was a major factor in achieving each artist's intention.

C

SCALE WITHIN ART

Scale can attract our attention in different ways, depending on the artist's purpose. Scale can be used to draw our notice to the unexpected or exaggerated, as when small objects are magnified or large ones reduced. The wash drawing in **A** is startling, as a tiny insect is now seen enlarged to page-filling size. Just the extreme change in scale attracts our attention.

The opposite approach is shown in **B**. Here the purposeful use of a very tiny subject in a vast, almost empty, space carries out the theme perfectly.

Unexpected scale is often used in advertising. As visual attention must be directed to a product, we regularly see lay-outs with a large package, cookie, automobile grille, cereal flake, or whatever. A sudden scale change surprises us and gets our attention.

The use of large or small scale is often employed in painting or design. However, a more common practice is to combine the two for a dramatic contrast. In the Degas painting **(C)** a very large-scale lady at the right is seated in her loge at the theater. On the background stage the figures gradually diminish in size as distance increases. Seeing a lady's fan far larger than a group of dancers provides scale contrast and visual interest.

A Mark Fennessey. *Insects IV*. 1965–66. Wash, 29 × 20″ (73.6 × 50.7 cm). Yale University Art Gallery (transfer from the Yale Art School).
B Book jacket, *Vanishing Breed*. Carl Zahn, Designer; Nan Jernigan, Art Director; William Albert Allard, Photographer. Courtesy Little, Brown and Co., Boston.
C Edgar Degas. *Dancer with a Bouquet of Flowers*. Ca. 1878–1880. Oil on canvas, 15⅞ × 19⅞″ (40 × 50 cm). Museum of Art, Rhode Island School of Design, Providence, RI (gift of Mrs. Murray S. Danforth).

A

B

VANISHING BREED
PHOTOGRAPHS OF THE COWBOY AND THE WEST
By William Albert Allard   Foreword by Thomas McGuane

VANISHING BREED

NY
GS

C

A

A René Magritte. *Personal Values*. 1952. Oil on canvas, 31⅝ × 39½″ (80 × 100 cm). Collection Harry Torczyner, New York.
B Eugeniusz Get-Staniewicz. *Self Portrait*. 1980. Reproduced from: ''Design in Poland,'' *Print* magazine, May/June 1992, p. 67. Courtesy of *Print*.
C Henry Koerner. *Mirror of Life*. 1946. Oil on composition board, 36 × 42″ (91.4 × 106.7 cm). Whitney Museum of American Art, New York (purchase, 48.2).

B

SCALE CONFUSION

The deliberate changing of natural scale is not unusual in painting. In religious paintings many artists have arbitrarily increased the size of the Christ or Virgin Mary figure to emphasize philosophic and religious importance.

Some artists, however, use scale changes intentionally to intrigue or mystify us, rather than to clarify the focal point. **Surrealism** is an art form based on paradox, on images that cannot be explained in rational terms. Artists who work in this manner present the irrational world of the dream or nightmare—recognizable elements in impossible situations. The painting by Magritte **(A)** shows one such enigma, with much of the mystery stemming from a confusion of scale. We identify the various elements easily enough, but they are all the "wrong" size and strange in proportion to each other. Does the painting show an impossibly large comb, shaving brush, bar of soap, and other items, or are these items normal size but placed in a dollhouse room? Neither explanation makes rational sense.

A scale change can feel very unsettling when applied to the human figure. The large eye within the triangle eclipses the "normal" eye in **B** and becomes the focus of this enigmatic and disturbing *Self Portrait*.

An arbitrary change of scale can have another visual surprise. We rather automatically associate size differences with space: Large items are closer to us, while smaller ones are farther away. But the intriguing painting in **C** challenges this size/distance relationship. The painting contains many small scenes. These are all painted in a very naturalistic manner so we can easily understand the images. But, spatially, their relative scale is very puzzling. Due to their sizes, some of these areas start to recede while others jump forward in a disconnected and incongruous manner across the painting. Again a painting with out-of-scale images produces a disconcerting result.

C

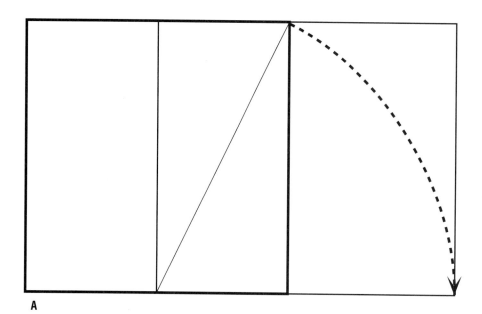

A A golden rectangle can be created by rotating the diagonal of the half-square.

B Parthenon, East Facade, Athens. The *root five* rectangle and *golden* rectangle are part of the geometry of the facade.

C Masaccio. *The Tribute Money*. Ca. 1427. Fresco, 8′4″ × 19′8″ (2.54 × 5.99 m). Santa Maria del Carmine, Florence. The geometry of *root five* and *golden* rectangles divides this three-part painting at significant locations.

B

PROPORTION

THE GOLDEN MEAN

Proportion is linked to ratio. That is to say we judge the proportions of something to be correct if the ratio of one element to another is correct. For example: the ratio of a baby's head size to its body size is in proportion for an infant, but would strike us as out of proportion for an adult. While we do not have universal rules for such proportions today, we still have a general idea of what is considered to be a normally proportioned body, and in a life drawing class you might learn that an adult is about seven-and-a-half heads tall.

The ancient Greeks had a desire to discover ideal proportions, and these took the form of mathematical ratios. They found the "perfect" body to be seven heads tall and even idealized the proportions of the parts of the body. In a similar fashion they sought perfect proportions in rectangles employed in architectural design. Among these rectangles the one most often cited as the perfect one is the **golden rectangle.** While this is certainly a subjective judgment, the golden rectangle has influenced art and design throughout the succeeding centuries.

The proportions of the golden rectangle can be expressed in the ratio of the parts to the whole. This ratio (called the ratio of the **golden mean**) is *width is to length as length is to length plus width* (w:1 as 1:1 + w). This rectangle can be created by rotating the diagonal of a half square as shown in **A**. Both the total rectangle created and the smaller rectangle attached to the square are golden rectangles in their proportions.

Further rotation of this diagonal describes a half circle and creates a new rectangle with a square at the center flanked by two golden rectangles. This rectangle can be seen in the facade of the Parthenon shown in **B**. The center square contains the four center columns.

This rectangle, a derivative of the golden rectangle, is called a *root 5 rectangle* because its proportions are $1:\sqrt{5}$. Masaccio's *Tribute Money* **(C)** exploits the properties of this rectangle in depicting a three-part narrative with grace and subtlety. In the center area (the square) the tax collector demands the tribute money from Christ, who instructs Peter to get the money from the fish's mouth. On the left Peter kneels to get the money, and on the right he pays the tax collector.

A number of contemporary artists and architects continue to use the proportions of the golden mean. There are other rectangles derived from the square, and other properties of the golden mean that can be studied in depth. These proportions do not provide a formula for design success. As with other visual principles the attributes of the golden mean offer an option for design exploration.

C

5

BALANCE

A

B

INTRODUCTION

The Dance Class **(A)** is a beautiful and intriguing painting. What makes it unusual concerns the principle of **balance** or distribution of visual weight within a composition. Here all the figures and visual attention seem concentrated on the left-hand side with the right-hand side basically empty. This is not what we expect to see. The effect seems a very spontaneous grouping, apparently unposed and momentary. The result looks like many of the unplanned, rather haphazard photographs we often take at parties or other events.

A sense of balance is innate; as children we develop a sense of balance in our bodies and observe balance in the world around us. Lack of balance, or **imbalance,** disturbs us. We observe momentary imbalance such as bodies engaged in active sports which quickly right themselves or fall. We carefully avoid dangerously leaning trees, rocks, furniture, and ladders. But even where no physical danger is present, as in a design or painting, we still feel more comfortable with a balanced pattern **(B)**.

In assessing pictorial balance, we always assume a center vertical axis and usually expect to see some kind of equal weight (visual weight) distribution on either side. This axis functions as the fulcrum on a scale or seesaw, and the two sides should achieve a sense of equilibrium. When this equilibrium is not present, as in **C**, a certain vague uneasiness or dissatisfaction results. We feel a need to rearrange the elements, in the same way that we automatically straighten a tilted picture on the wall.

A Edgar Degas. *École de Danse.* Ca. 1875. Oil and tempera on canvas, 17¼ × 23″ (44 × 58 cm). Shelburne Museum, Shelburne, VT.

B John Trumbull. *The Surrender of Lord Cornwallis.* 1787–1794. Oil on canvas, 20⅞ × 30⅝″ (53 × 78 cm). Copyright Yale University Art Gallery, New Haven, CT.

C An unbalanced design leaves the viewer with a vague uneasiness.

C

A

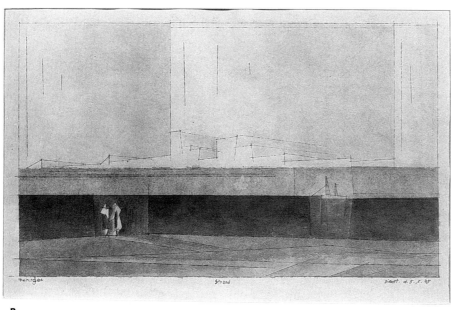

B

C

A Thomas Wilmer Dewing. *The Piano.* Ca. 1891. Oil on panel, 20 × 26½″ (50.8 × 67.5 cm). © Smithsonian Institution, Courtesy of the Freer Gallery of Art.

B Lyonel Feininger. *Strand.* 1925. Watercolor and pen and ink on pulp paper, 11⁹⁄₁₆ × 17″ (29.4 × 43.2 cm). The Brooklyn Museum (Museum Collection Fund, 31.128).

C Paul Klee. *Tightrope Walker,* plate 4 from the portfolio *Mappe der Gegenwart.* 1923. Color lithograph, 17⅛ × 10⅝″ (44 × 26 cm). The Museum of Modern Art, New York (given anonymously).

D Marc Chagall. *Over Vitebsk.* 1915–20 (after a painting of 1914). Oil on canvas, 26⅜ × 36½″ (67 × 93 cm). The Museum of Modern Art, New York (acquired through the Lillie P. Bliss Bequest).

INTRODUCTION

Balance—some equal distribution of visual weight—is a universal aim of composition. The vast majority of pictures we see have been consciously balanced by the artist. However, this does not mean there is no place in art for purposeful imbalance. An artist may, because of a particular theme or topic, expressly desire that a picture raise uneasy, disquieting responses in the viewer. In this instance imbalance can be a useful tool. Even without such a motive, an occasional imbalanced image, such as that in the Dewing painting **(A)** interests us and attracts our attention for this unexpected quality.

In speaking of pictorial balance, we are almost always referring to horizontal balance, the right and left sides of the image. Artists consider vertical balance as well, with a horizontal axis dividing top and bottom. Again, a certain general equilibrium is usually desirable. However, because of our sense of gravity, we are accustomed to seeing more weight toward the bottom, with a resulting stability and calm **(B)**. The farther up in the format the main distribution of weight or visual interest occurs, the more unstable and dynamic the image becomes.

The effect can be seen in Paul Klee's whimsical *Tightrope Walker* **(C)**; the instability of the image expresses the theme perfectly. The linear patterns build up vertically until we reach the teetering figure near the top. The artist can manipulate the vertical balance freely to fit a particular theme or purpose.

The Chagall painting **(D)** has emphasis at the top. The dark buildings and especially the floating figure in the sky give emphasis to the upper half of the composition.

D

A

B

A Man's shirt (front view), Chilkat, Alaska. Ca. 1890–1900. Woven from goats hair on a cedarbark base, 44¾″ (114 cm) long. National Museum of the American Indian, Smithsonian Institution (#20961).

B Henry N. Cobb/I. M. Pei and Partners. Portland Museum of Art, Portland, ME. 1983.

C Alessandro Tremignon. San Moise Cathedral, Venice. Ca. 1688.

SYMMETRICAL BALANCE

The simplest type of balance, both to create and to recognize, is called **symmetrical balance.** In symmetrical balance, like shapes are repeated in the same positions on either side of a vertical axis. One side, in effect, becomes the mirror image of the other side. Symmetrical balance has a seemingly basic appeal for us, which can be ascribed to the awareness of our bodies' essential symmetry. In the case of the shirt shown in **A** the symmetry is clearly in response to this symmetry of the body.

Conscious symmetrical repetition, while clearly creating perfect balance, can be undeniably static, so that the term **formal balance** is used to describe the same idea. There is nothing wrong with quiet formality. In fact, this characteristic is often desired in some art, notably in architecture. Countless examples of architecture with symmetrical balance can be found throughout the world, dating from most periods of art history. The continuous popularity of symmetrical design is not hard to understand. The formal quality in symmetry imparts an immediate feeling of permanence, strength, and stability. Such quali-

ties are important in public buildings to suggest the dignity and power of a government. So statehouses, city halls, palaces, courthouses, and other government monuments often exploit the properties of symmetrical balance.

The art museum in Portland, Maine **(B)** has a rigidly repetitive pattern, and the result is a sedate, calm, and dignified facade. Such an effect is often termed classical, alluding to the many ancient Greek and Roman buildings in which symmetrical design imparted the same feeling of clarity and rational order.

Symmetrical balance does not, by itself, preordain any specific visual result. Examples **B** and **C** are both symmetrical facades, but here the similarity ends. The stark simplicity of the museum **(B)** with the orderly progression of a few repeated shapes and a calm, regular rhythm of dark and light is certainly not present in the Italian cathedral **(C)**. The latter is a busy, exciting, ornate building with only the symmetrical organization molding the masses of niches, columns, and statuary into a unified and coherent visual pattern.

C

SYMMETRICAL BALANCE

Symmetrical balance is rarer in painting than in architecture. In fact, relatively few paintings would fit a strict definition of symmetry.

Sometimes the subject matter of a painting makes symmetrical balance an appropriate compositional device. A dignified, solemn subject such as the Madonna enthroned **(A)** clearly calls for the stable, calm qualities symmetrical balance can impart. In this example, while the architectural setting is completely symmetrical, the saints flanking the Madonna are similar but not identical.

Barbara Kruger's *Why Are You Here?* **(B)** exploits the symmetry of the human face. She accentuates it with the gesture of the hands grabbing and bracketing the head. In this case the figure provides symmetry in an architectural setting that is asymmetrical. This large billboard-like image is at the bottom of the staircase leading to an art center's exhibition galleries.

The symmetry of the image reinforces the bold type and insistent question that confronts the viewer.

Both **A** and **B** show one distinct advantage to symmetrical compositions: the immediate creation and emphasis of a focal point. With the two sides being so much alike, there is an obvious visual importance to whatever element is placed on the center axis.

Margaret Wharton transforms a wooden chair into a *Mocking Bird* **(C)** through a process of slicing and reassembling. In this case we can, once again, trace the origins of the sculpture's symmetry back to the human figure. The symmetry of the chair derives from the human body for which it is designed. Wharton's cut and reassembled version takes on the winged symmetry of a bird-like form. In this case symmetry results in a whimsical, light-hearted artwork, rather than a solemn or insistent image.

A

B

A Domenico Veneziano. *The St. Lucy Altarpiece.* Ca.
1445. Tempera on wood panel, approx. 6'7½" × 7'
(2.02 × 2.13 m). Galleria degli Uffizi, Florence.

B Barbara Kruger. *Why Are You Here?* 1990 Silkscreen
on paper, 191 × 148" (4.8 × 3.8 m). Installation,
Wexner Center for the Arts, Ohio State University;
© Barbara Kruger.

C Margaret Wharton. *Mocking Bird.* 1981. Partially
stained wooden chair, epoxy glue, paint and wooden
dowels, 60 × 60 × 13" (152 × 152 × 33 cm).
Courtesy of the artist and Zolla/Lieberman Gallery,
Chicago.

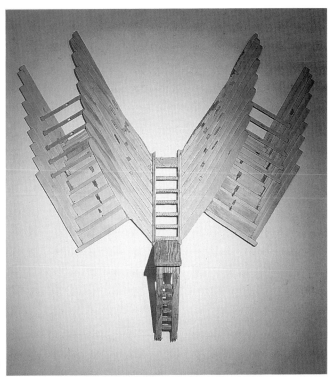

C

A S Y M M E T R I C A L   B A L A N C E

INTRODUCTION

The second type of balance is called **asymmetrical balance.** In this case balance is achieved with *dissimilar* objects that have equal visual weight or equal eye attraction. Remember the children's riddle: ''Which weighs more, a pound of feathers of a pound of lead?'' Of course, they both weigh a pound, but the amount and mass of each vary radically. This, then, is the essence of asymmetrical balance.

In Käthe Kollwitz's drawing **(A)** the child gazes out at us from the left side of the picture. But the composition is not off-balance. The right side is dominated by the lamp which illuminates the scene. The two sides of the picture are thus very different, with quite dissimilar elements, yet a sense of balance is maintained as each side provides a visual emphasis.

Kollwitz's drawing shows one advantage of asymmetrical balance. It is casual, not contrived or posed in feeling. The alternate title **informal balance** is often used, and the term is appropriate. This painting is informal. This feeling stems not solely from the child in the momentary act of looking toward the viewer, but from the whole composition that, at first glance, appears completely natural and spontaneous.

Symmetry can appear artificial, as our visual experiences in life are rarely symmetrically arranged. Some buildings and interiors are so designed, but even here, unless we stand quietly at dead center, our views are always asymmetrical.

Asymmetry appears casual and less planned, although obviously this characteristic is misleading. Asymmetrical balance is actually more intricate and complicated to use than symmetrical balance. Merely repeating similar elements in a mirror image on either side of the center is not a difficult design task. But attempting to balance *dis*similar items involves more complex considerations and more subtle factors.

The contrast possible in asymmetrical balance can be seen in **B**. This Tokyo building is a combination office and living space. On a small scale, a great contrast of bold elements in asymmetrical balance creates a dynamic visual pattern. On the left is a large, plain wall of horizontal tiles, which shields the spaces behind it. On the right an unexpected dark wedge juts out over the geometric lower office entrance. A gold, accordion-pleated element connects the two areas. Balance is achieved with very dissimilar elements.

The sculpture by Haim Steinbach **(C)** shows how ''two'' can balance ''three'' in an asymmetric arrangement. Two black pitchers sit on a red shelf adjacent to three red ''Bold 3'' boxes on a black shelf. This asymmetric pairing invites us to find the visual rhymes and contrasts that exist across the dividing line. The visual interest in comparing the unequal sides results in a balanced composition, and the number of elements feels correct.

A Käthe Kollwitz. *Mother and Child by Lamplight at the Table (Self Portrait with Son, Hans?).* 1894. Pen and ink with brush and wash, 8 × 10⅝" (21 × 27 cm). Sächsische Landesbibliothek, Deutsche Fotothek Dresden.

B Atsushi Kitagawara/ILCD, Inc. 395 Minami-Aoyama, Tokyo.

C Haim Steinbach. *supremely black.* 1989. Mixed media construction, 29 × 66 × 13" (74 × 168 × 33 cm). Courtesy Sonnabend Gallery and Jay Gorney Modern Art, New York.

A

B

C

ASYMMETRICAL BALANCE

BALANCE BY VALUE AND COLOR

Asymmetrical balance is based on equal eye attraction—dissimilar objects are equally interesting to the eye. One element that attracts our attention is **value** difference, a contrast of light and dark. Example **A** illustrates that black against white gives a stronger contrast than gray against white; therefore, a smaller amount of black is needed to visually balance a larger amount of gray.

The nineteenth-century woodcut in **B** shows the idea. The obvious subject is the lovers who are on the left side of the composition. They are visually balanced on the right by the stark white area of the tablecloth against a black background.

The photograph of the cathedral at York **(C)** reverses the values but shows the same balance technique. The left side of the composition shows many details of the angled wall of the church nave. However, the receding arches, piers, columns, and so on, are shown in subtle gradations of gray, all very close and related in value. In contrast, on the right side is the large black silhouette of a foreground column and the small window

area of bright white. These two sharp visual accents of white and black are on the right and balance the many, essentially gray, elements on the left.

A seventeenth-century painting **(D)** groups many items on the left side. There are far fewer on the right, but the sharp black-and-white value contrast of the "chequerboard" squares attracts the eye and balances the painting.

Like value contrast, color itself can be a balancing element. Studies have proven that our eyes are attracted to color. Given a choice, we will always look at a colored image rather than at one in black and white. A small area of bright color can balance a much larger area of a duller, more neutral color. Our eyes, drawn by the color, see the smaller element to be as interesting and as "heavy" visually as the larger element.

Balance by value or color is a great tool, allowing a great difference of shapes on either side of the center axis and still achieving equal eye attraction.

SEE ALSO: *Color and Balance, page 240.*

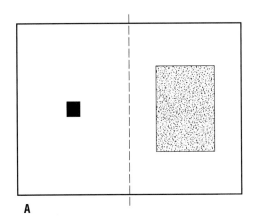

A

B

C

A A darker, smaller element is visually equal to a lighter, larger one.
B Felix Vallotton. *The Lie.* 1897. Plate I from *Les Intimités,* Godefroy 186, woodcut printed in black. Photograph courtesy of The Art Institute of Chicago (gift of the Print and Drawing Club, 1948.3.1).
C Frederic H. Evans. *York Minster, Into the South Transept.* Ca. 1900. Platinum print mounted on a sheet of brown paper upon a natural Japanese paper upon a larger sheet of gray paper. 8¼ × 4¾″ (20.9 × 12.1 cm). Metropolitan Museum of Art, New York (Alfred Stieglitz Collection, 33.43.368).
D Baugin. *Still Life with a Chequerboard (The Five Senses).* Ca. 1630. Oil on panel, 21¾ × 28¾″(55 × 73 cm). Musée du Louvre, Paris.

D

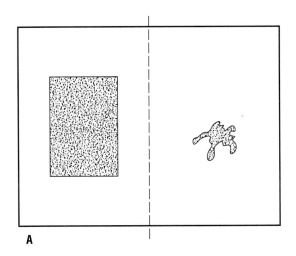

A

B

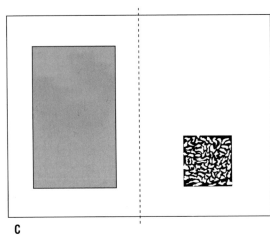

C

ASYMMETRICAL BALANCE

BALANCE BY SHAPE AND TEXTURE

The diagram in **A** illustrates balance by shape. Here the two elements are exactly the same value and texture. The only difference is their shape. The smaller form attracts the eye because of its more complicated contours. Though small, it is as interesting as the much larger, but duller, rectangle.

The balance of the elements in the Japanese woodcut **(B)** shows how a large simple form can be balanced by an intricate pattern or texture. The large simple triangular mass of the mountain is positioned to the right. The left side is balanced by the smaller, busy shapes of the clouds and the mass of small dark triangles that suggests a forest of trees. Even the symbols of the artist's signature marks provide balance on the left.

Any visual texture with a variegated dark and light pattern holds more interest for the eye than does a smooth, unrelieved surface. The drawing in **C** presents this idea: The smaller, rough-textured area balances the larger, basically untextured area (smoothness is, in a sense, a "texture").

The two figures on the left side of Mary Cassatt's painting **(D)** attract our attention and are obviously the emphasis of the composition. The picture is balanced, however, by the texture of the tea service on the right. The depiction of the reflective surface catches our eye with its pattern of lights and darks.

Printed text consisting of letters and words in effect creates a visual texture. The information is in symbols that we can read, but the visual effect is nothing more than a gray-patterned shape. Depending on the typeface and the layout, this gray area varies in darkness, density, and character, but it is visually textured. Very often in advertisements or editorial page layouts an area of "textured" printed matter will balance an element.

A A small, complicated shape is balanced by a larger, more stable shape.

B Katsushika Hokusai. *Fuji in Clear Weather* from *Thirty-Six Views of Fuji*. Ca. 1820–1830. Color woodcut, 10 × 15″ (25 × 28 cm). Metropolitan Museum of Art, New York (bequest of Henry L. Phillips, 1939; JP 2960).

C A small textured shape can balance a larger untextured one.

D Mary Stevenson Cassatt. *Five O'Clock Tea.* Ca. 1880. Oil on canvas, 25½ × 36½″ (65 × 93 cm). Courtesy, Museum of Fine Arts, Boston (M. Theresa B. Hopkins Fund).

D

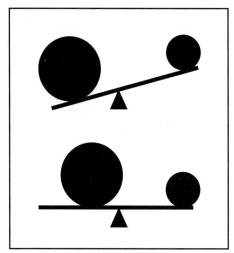

A

B

ASYMMETRICAL BALANCE

BALANCE BY POSITION AND EYE DIRECTION

The two seesaw diagrams in **A** illustrate the idea of **balance by position.** A well-known principle in physics is that two items of unequal weight can be brought to equilibrium by moving the heavier inward toward the fulcrum. In design this means that a large item placed closer to the center can be balanced by a smaller item placed out toward the edge.

Balance by position often lends an unusual, unexpected quality to the composition. The effect not only appears casual and unplanned, but also can make the composition seem, at first glance, to be in imbalance. This casual impression can be seen in the illustration by Aubrey Beardsley **(B)**. The fat, pompous figure strides on stage from the left. It is visually balanced by the small child peeking out from under the curtain at the far right edge. The effect is emphasized by the rigidly symmetrical design at the bottom.

One further element in achieving asymmetrical balance should be noted. Often the many heavier elements can direct our attention to the opposite side, thus making small elements a balancing element. The technique is used in the Art Deco railway poster **(C)**. The large, dark locomotive is positioned on the left, but the accentuated perspective lines of the receding train and platform make a sharp arrow that directs attention to the right. Actually, only a few lines of the distant station and the tiny engineer's figure are on the right side, but the eye direction creates the optical balance.

While not usually the *only* technique of balance employed, the useful device of eye direction is commonly used by artists. Eye direction is carefully plotted, not only for balance but also for general compositional unity.

A A large shape placed near the middle of a design can be balanced by a smaller shape placed toward the outer edge.
B Aubrey Beardsley. *Design for the Prospectus of ''The Savoy''.* 1895.
C Pierre Fix-Masseau. *Exactitude.* Gouache, after a poster of 1929, 39⅜ × 24½" (100 × 62 cm). Metropolitan Museum of Art, New York (gift of the Publisher's Office, 1983.1014).

C

ASYMMETRICAL BALANCE

ANALYSIS SUMMARY

In looking at paintings, you will realize that isolating one technique of asymmetrical balance as we have done is a bit misleading, since the vast majority of works employ several of the methods simultaneously. For the sake of clarity these methods are discussed separately, but the principles often overlap and are frequently used together. Let us look at just a few examples that make use of several of the factors involved in asymmetrical balance.

The painting by Carel Willink (**A**) would appear, at first glance, to be unbalanced, as the large, dominant building is on the right side of the composition. A number of elements work to balance this point of emphasis. Perspective lines in the architecture and the street lead our eye to the distant (and therefore smaller) image of a building on the left. The left side of the painting also includes the dramatic pattern of the light breaking

through the clouds. Together, these aspects of the picture provide a counterweight to the building in the foreground.

The title of Martin Puryear's sculpture shown in **B** is appropriate for the asymmetric balance that is achieved. *Lever No. 3* presents a quirky and unexpected form with a small circular loop cast off from a more massive body. This loop sits like a head atop a long neck and visually balances the weight of the grounded body. The effect is like that of the smaller weight at the end of a long lever arm, but our visual interest is drawn to the space inside the loop more powerfully than if it were simply a solid circle. This added complexity helps offset the much larger bulk of the right side.

The figure in the Japanese print shown in **C** holds out a lantern in a manner that is surprisingly reminiscent of Puryear's sculpture. This picture, however, contains more elements. Notice how shape, value, position, and eye direction are all involved in balancing the composition.

A

B

A Carel Willink. *Townview*. 1934. Oil on canvas, 29½ × 39½″ (75 × 100.5 cm). Stedelijk Van Abbemuseum, Eindhoven.

B Martin Puryear. *Lever No. 3*. 1989. Wood, carved and painted, 84½ × 162 × 13″ (2.15 m × 4.12 m × 33 cm). © 1993 National Gallery of Art, Washington, DC (gift of the Collectors Committee).

C Suzuki Harunobu. *Girl with Lantern on Balcony at Night*. Ca. 1768. Color woodcut, 12¾ × 8¼″ (32 × 21 cm). Metropolitan Museum of Art, New York (Fletcher Fund, 1929; JP 150).

C

RADIAL BALANCE

A third variety of balance is called **radial balance.** Here all the elements radiate or circle out from a common central point. The sun with its emanating rays is a familiar symbol that expresses the basic idea. Radial balance is not entirely distinct from symmetrical or asymmetrical balance. It is merely a refinement of one or the other, depending on whether the focus occurs in the middle or off center.

Circular forms abound in craft areas, where the round shapes of ceramics, basketry, and jewelry often make radial balance a natural choice in decorating such objects. Radial balance has been used frequently in architecture. The round form of domed buildings such as the Roman Pantheon or our nation's Capitol will almost automatically give a radial feeling to the interior.

It is true that in narrative Western painting, pure radial designs are uncommon. But in other cultures and in other design applications, radial patterns are often seen. The design in **A** is a *mandala* from Tibet. For centuries in the Buddhist man-

dala, various gods have been shown in a radial concentric organization of geometric shapes. The radial balance is a traditional device.

The major compositional advantage in radial balance is the immediate and obvious creation of a focal point. Perhaps this is also the reason that such balance seldom occurs in painting. It might seem a little too contrived and unnatural, a little too obvious to be entirely satisfactory. But this is the very reason why it can be useful in other design areas. For example, in advertising, where there is a visual need to emphasize a product, a picture, or a headline **(B)**, a radial composition uses many elements to direct the viewer's eye to the one important element.

The dramatic painting by Judy Chicago **(C)** is clearly a radial pattern. The abstracted forms have a feeling of flower shapes and also (as intended) are suggestive of the theme of feminine sexuality.

A

B

C

A *Mandala de Vaicravana,* Tibet. Musée Guimet, Paris.

B Advertisement for Zwilling Cutlery. Dentsu Advertising Agency, Osaka, Japan; Art Director/Copywriter: Wataru Ashida; Photographer: Nob Fukuda.

C Judy Chicago. *Rejection Quintet: Female Rejection Drawing.* 1974. Prismacolor and graphite on rag / board, 39⅝ × 29⅝″ (101 × 75 cm). San Francisco Museum of Modern Art (gift of Tracy O'Kates).

CRYSTALLOGRAPHIC BALANCE

ALLOVER PATTERN

One more specific type of visual effect is often designated as a fourth variety of balance. The examples here illustrate the idea. These works all exhibit an equal emphasis over the whole format—the same weight or eye attraction literally everywhere.

This technique is officially called **crystallographic balance.** Since few people can remember this term, and even fewer can spell it, the more common name is **allover pattern.** This is, of course, a rather special refinement of symmetrical balance. The constant repetition of the same quality everywhere on the surface, however, is truly a different impression from our usual concept of symmetrical balance.

In Alfred Jensen's painting **(A)**, emphasis is uniform throughout. The many numbers appear in the same size, with each defined in the same thick brushstroke and paint texture. Value changes are interesting but are also quite evenly distributed. There is no beginning, no end, and no focal point—unless, indeed, the whole picture is the focal point.

Traditional quilt patterns are often distinguished by a constant repetition of the same motif. Patterns such as ''baby-blocks'' (which creates an illusion of stacked blocks) or ''fans in a drunkard's path'' (a fan pattern which creates ''s'' curves) playfully repeat the same basic unit. The contemporary quilt in **B** repeats diamonds and triangles; however, the pattern of lights and darks does not repeat in a constant manner. The total effect is still of an allover composition with an equal emphasis and weight across the entire surface.

Both **A** and **B** are quite active visual patterns, with a variety of forms. This is not, of course, always true of crystallographic designs. The drawing by Eva Hesse **(C)** is very simple. The whole composition consists of the repetition of target-like circles in graduated values. The circles are distributed evenly throughout the design by their placement on a grid. There is no point of emphasis, and we are left to ponder the subtle nuances of this quiet, simple structure.

A

B

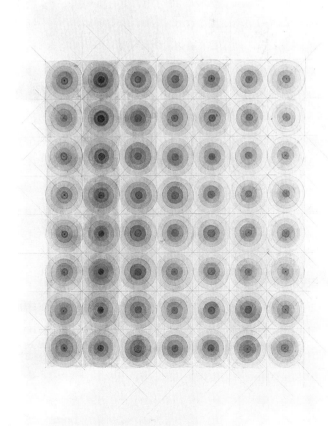

A Alfred Jensen. *Coordinative Thinking on the Square and Rectangle; Per, IV.* 1974. Oil and felt tip pen ink on board, 30 × 22″ (76.2 × 56 cm). San Francisco Museum of Modern Art (gift of Sam Francis).

B Nancy Crow. *Jacob's Ladder #1.* 1986. Cotton quilt, 58 × 70″ (147 × 178 cm). © Nancy Crow, 1986.

C Eva Hesse. *Untitled.* 1966. Pencil, wash, and brush on paper, 11⅞ × 9⅛″ (30 × 23 cm). The Museum of Modern Art, New York (gift of Mr. and Mrs. Herbert Fischbach).

C

6

RHYTHM

INTRODUCTION

In conversation we might refer to Bridget Riley's painting in **A** as having a *rhythmic* feeling. This might seem a strange adjective to use because **rhythm** is a term we most often associate with the sense of hearing. Without words, music can intrigue us by its pulsating beat, inducing us to tap a foot or perhaps dance. Poetry often has *meter,* which is a term for measurable rhythm. The pace of words can establish a cadence, a repetitive flow of syllables that makes reading poems aloud a pleasure. But rhythm can also be a visual sensation. We commonly speak of rhythm when watching the movement displayed by athletes, dancers, or some workers performing manual tasks. In a similar way the quality of rhythm can be applied to the visual arts, in which the idea is again basically related to movement. Here the concept refers to the movement of the viewer's eye, a movement across recurrent motifs providing the repetition inherent in the idea of rhythm. The painting in **A** has this feeling of repetition in the softly flowing vertical forms. It is not necessarily the nonobjective nature of the shapes that produces this feeling. A similar effect is present in the photograph shown in **B**. Now tree trunks show the same sinuous and graceful rhythm.

Rhythm as a design principle is based on repetition. Repetition, as an element of visual unity, is exhibited in some manner by almost every work of art. However, rhythm involves a clear repetition of elements that are the same or only slightly modified.

The paintings in **A** and **C** are similar in many ways. Both are devoid of subject matter and present a similar pattern of vertical elements extending across the canvas. But we can sense a subtle difference in the rhythm expressed. The smooth, flowing quality of **A** is not present in the rigid, sharp verticals of the painting by Gene Davis (**C**). The rhythm here seems harder, with crisp elements of stress and pause, almost like a drum sounding an irregular pattern of loud and soft beats.

The senses of sight and hearing are indeed so closely allied that we often relate them by interchanging adjectives (such as ''loud'' and ''soft'' colors). Certainly this relationship is shown in the concept of visual rhythm.

A

B

A Bridget Riley. *Drift No. 2*. 1966. Acrylic on canvas, 7′7½″ × 7′5½″ (2.32 × 2.27 m). Albright-Knox Art Gallery, Buffalo, NY (gift of Seymour H. Knox, 1967).

B Albert Renger-Patzsch. *Buchenwald in Fall (or Trees)*. 1936. Gelatin silver print, 9 × 6⅝″ (22.9 × 16.8 cm). Metropolitan Museum of Art, New York (Warner Communications, Inc., purchase fund, 1978; 1980.1063.1).

C Gene Davis. *Billy Budd*. 1964. Acrylic on canvas, 5′8½″ × 6′4⅞″ (1.74 × 1.95 m). Charles Cowles Gallery, New York.

C

A

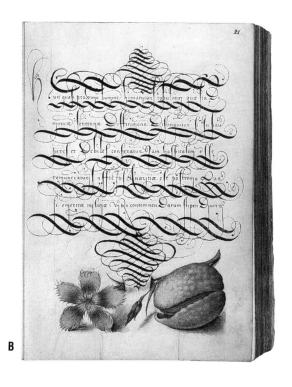

B

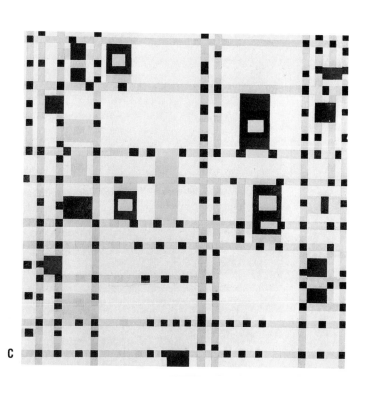

C

RHYTHM AND MOTION

We may speak of the rhythmic repetition of colors or textures, but most often we think of rhythm in the context of shapes and their arrangement. In music, some rhythms are called **legato,** or connecting and slowing. The same word could easily be applied to the visual effect in **A**. The photograph of Death Valley shows the sand dune ridges in undulating, flowing, horizontal curves. The dark and light contrast is quite dramatic, but in several places the changes are soft with smooth transitions. The feeling is relaxing and calm.

A similar rhythm occurs in the sixteenth-century illuminated manuscript by Hoefnagel (**B**). Here the rhythm is faster with more repetitions and more regularity or consistency in the repeated curves. The fluid strokes carry our eye across the text and mark both the beginning and end of the passage with a flourish.

It is true that the rhythmic pattern an artist chooses can very quickly establish an emotional response in the viewer. For contrast, look at the painting in **C**. The effect here is also rhythmic, but now of an entirely different sort. Small, bold, sharply dark squares move horizontally and vertically around the light canvas. The shapes are rigidly defined with the value changes

sudden and startling. Again, music has a term for this type of rhythm: **staccato,** meaning abrupt changes with a dynamic contrast. The recurrence of these dark squares establishes a visual rhythm. The irregular spacing of the small squares causes the pattern (and rhythm) to be lively rather than monotonous. The artist, Piet Mondrian, titled this painting *Broadway Boogie-Woogie.* He has expressed in the most abstract visual terms not only the on/off patterns of Broadway's neon landscape but also the rhythmic sounds of 1940s instrumental blues music. The effect for us today is almost like the jumpy, always changing patterns we see in video games.

The rhythms of **A** and **C** are indeed different, but the two examples are also alike in that the rhythm initially established is then consistent and regular throughout the composition. This regularity is not present in Gregory Amenoff's painting (**D**). The eye moves through repeated bent or angular elements, but the points of emphasis are in an irregular pattern. We are pushed and pulled in various directions. Our eyes are jerked quickly back and forth across the composition; the rhythm is exciting but also unsettling.

A   Bruce Barnbaum. *Dune Ridges at Sunrise, Death Valley.* 1976. Silver gelatin print, 10¾ × 13¼″ (27.3 × 33.6 cm). Courtesy the photographer.

B   Georg Hoefnagel (illuminator) and Georg Bocskay (scribe). *Mira Calligraphiae Monumenta (Model Book of Calligraphy),* Fols. 1–129; *A Guide to the Construction of the Letters of the Alphabet,* Fols. 130– 151. 1561–62. Pen and ink, watercolors on vellum and paper, 6⁹⁄₁₆ × 4¹³⁄₁₆″ (16.6 × 12.3 cm). Collection of the J. Paul Getty Museum, Malibu, CA (86.MV.527, fol. 21r).

C   Piet Mondrian. *Broadway Boogie-Woogie.* 1942– 1943. Oil on canvas, 50 × 50″ (127 × 127 cm). The Museum of Modern Art, New York (given anonymously).

D   Gregory Amenoff. *Out of the Blue and into the Black.* 1979. Oil on canvas, 60 × 84″ (1.5 × 2.1 m). Collection of Leonard F., Cheryl Y., Alys R., Daya A., Jairus and Tucker Yablon, Steelton, PA.

D

ALTERNATING RHYTHM

Rhythm is a basic characteristic of nature. The pattern of the seasons, of day and night, of the tides, and even of the movements of the planets, all exhibit a regular rhythm. This rhythm consists of successive patterns in which the same elements reappear in a regular order. In a design or painting this would be termed an **alternating rhythm,** as motifs alternate consistently with one another to produce a regular (and anticipated) sequence. This expected quality of the pattern is not a fault, for unless he repetition is fairly obvious, the whole idea of visual rhythm becomes obscure.

A familiar example of this idea can be seen in a building with columns, such as a Greek temple. The repeating pattern of light columns against darker negative spaces is clearly an alternating rhythm. Architectural critics often speak of the "rhyth-mic" placement of windows on a facade. Again it is an alternating pattern—dark glass against a solid wall. The exterior stairway of Le Corbusier's building **(A)** shows this type of rhythm. The design involves a sequence of forms that not only alternate in dark and light areas, but shift regularly back and forth from straight edges to curves.

Notice that exactly the same description of alternating themes could be used for the painting in **B**. The artist, Robert Delaunay, titled this work, appropriately, *Rhythm Without End.*

The light and dark areas alternate consistently in Ansel Adams' photograph **(C)**. The everyday scene of political (and circus) posters pasted on a corrugated iron wall shows the regular value variation we associate with alternating rhythm.

A Le Corbusier. Unité d'Habitation. 1947–1952. External escape stairway, Marseilles.

B Robert Delaunay. *Rhythm Without End.* 1935. Gouache, brush and ink, 10⅝ × 8¼″ (27 × 21 cm). The Museum of Modern Art, New York (given anonymously).

C Ansel Adams. *Political Sign and Circus Posters, San Francisco.* 1931. Photograph. Copyright © 1993 by the Trustees of the Ansel Adams Publishing Rights Trust. All Rights Reserved.

A

B

C

A

A Edward Ruscha. *Good Year Tires, 6610 Laurel Canyon, North Hollywood.* 1967. Photograph, 8¼ × 3⅞″ (21 × 10 cm). From the book *Thirty-four Parking Lots in Los Angeles.*

B Edward Weston. *Artichoke, Halved.* 1930. Gelatin silver print, 7½ × 9½″ (19 × 24.1 cm). © 1981, Center for Creative Photography, Arizona Board of Regents.

Progressive Rhythm

Another type of rhythm is called **progression, or progressive rhythm.** Again, the rhythm involves repetition, but repetition of a shape that changes in a regular manner. There is a feeling of a sequential pattern. This type of rhythm is most often achieved with a progressive variation of the size of a shape, though its color, value, or texture could be the varying element. Progressive rhythm is extremely familiar to us; we experience it daily when we look at buildings from an angle. The perspective changes the horizontals and verticals into a converging pattern that creates a regular sequence of shapes gradually diminishing in size.

In **A** the rhythmic sequence of lines moving vertically across the format is immediately obvious. A more subtle progressive rhythm appears when we notice the dark shapes of the oil stains in the parking spaces. These change in size, becoming progressively smaller further away from the building. In this photograph from an aerial vantage point, a rhythm is revealed in the ordinary pattern of human habits.

Progressive rhythms are actually rather commonplace in nature although they may not always be readily apparent. Edward Weston's extreme closeup of an artichoke cut in half **(B)** shows a growth pattern. The gradual increase in size and weight creates a visual movement upward and outward. Other natural forms (such as a chambered nautilus shell) cut in cross section would also reveal progressive rhythms.

The photographs in **A** and **B** are quite different. Yet they both make visible progressive rhythms from the world around us, whether in the pattern of human activity or in natural forms.

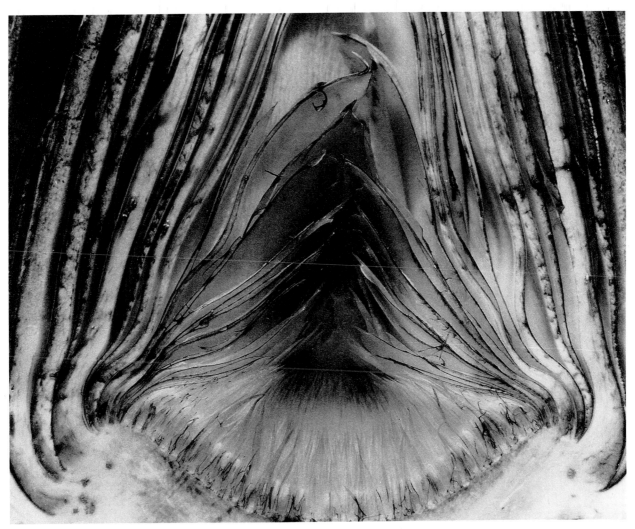

B

A

A Charles Burchfield. *The Insect Chorus.* 1917. Opaque
and transparent watercolor with ink and crayon on
paper, 19⅞ × 15⅞″ (50 × 40 cm). Munson-Williams-
Proctor Institute, Museum of Art, Utica, New York
(Edward W. Root Bequest).

B Kasimir Malevich. *Suprematist Composition:
Sensation of Metallic Sounds.* 1916–18. Crayon on
paper, 8 × 6½″ (20.9 × 16.4 cm). Öffentliche
Kunstsammlung Basel, Kupferstichkabinett.

C Kasimir Malevich. *Suprematist Composition:
Sensation of Movement and Resistance.* Crayon on
paper, 10½ × 8″ (26.5 × 20.5 cm). Öffentliche
Kunstsammlung Basel, Kupferstichkabinett.

RHYTHMIC SENSATIONS

Rhythmic structures in visual art and design are often described (as they have been here) in terms borrowed from the vocabulary of music. The connection between visual rhythms and musical rhythms can be more than a simile or metaphor. In some cases the visual rhythms composed by an artist seem to resonate with memories or associations in our other senses. When a visual experience actually stimulates one of our other senses, the effect is called **kinaesthetic.**

Charles Burchfield's painting **(A)** is, on one level, a depiction of the roofline of a building set among trees and plants. This description does not tell us the subject of *The Insect Chorus,* however. A description of the painting's many rhythmic patterns would come closer to explaining the title. Repeated curves, zig-zags, and straight linear elements throughout the picture literally buzz and create the sensation of a hot summer afternoon alive with the sound of cicadas. Even the sensation of heat is evoked by the rhythm of wavering lines above the rooftop.

The drawing shown in **B** attempts to convey the sensation of "metallic sounds." This early experiment in Russian Suprematist Art from 1918 reflects the interest in industrial subjects of that era. The jumpy arrangement of shapes, almost lacking in any rhythmic pattern, seems to echo the harsh, dynamic sounds of a factory.

A second drawing by Malevich **(C)** is titled *The Sensation of Movement and Resistance.* In this case our physical experiences of moving through the world are simulated. The drawing appeals to our sense of touch and "muscle memory" by repeating horizontal lines of varying weight along a curved path. The rhythmic interruption of the heavier, darker rectangles offers the "resistance" referred to in the title.

B

C

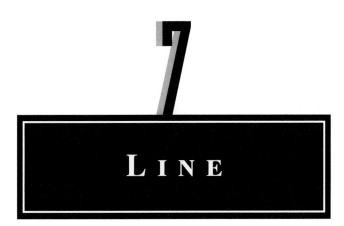

7

LINE

INTRODUCTION

Of all the elements in art, **line** is the most familiar to us. Most of our writing and drawing tools are pointed, and we have been making lines constantly since we were young children. Most of the cartoons we see daily in our newspapers are simple line drawings **(A)**.

What is a line? Other than a mark made by a pointed tool, a line is a form that has length and width, but the width is so tiny compared to the length that we perceive the line as having only the latter dimension. Geometry defines a line as an infinite number of points. The usual art definition of a line is a moving dot. This latter definition is useful to remember because it recognizes the inherent dynamic quality of line. A line is created by movement. Since our eyes must follow it, a line's potential to suggest motion is basic. The impression of movement we feel when looking at the drawing *Fright* **(B)** shows the idea

clearly. The artist's line seems to be moving and recoiling before our eyes. The quivering quality of the line technique expresses the theme of the drawing.

Line is capable of infinite variety. Example **C** shows just a few of the almost unlimited variations possible in the category of line. A curious feature of line is its power of suggestion. What an expressive tool it can be for the artist! A line is a minimum statement, made quickly with a minimum of effort, but seemingly able to convey all sorts of moods and feelings. The lines pictured in **C** are truly abstract shapes: they depict no objects. Yet we can read into them emotional and expressive qualities. Think of all the adjectives we can apply to lines. We often describe lines as being nervous, angry, happy, free, quiet, excited, calm, graceful, dancing, and having many other qualities. The power of suggestion of this basic element is great.

A

I'm sorry, sir, you're overdrawn

B

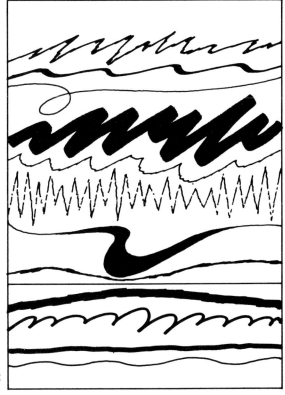

A Gumpertz. *I'm Sorry, Sir, You're Overdrawn*. 1986.
© Robert Gumpertz.

B Honoré Daumier. *Fright*. 1828–79. Charcoal with
black crayon, on ivory laid paper, 8 × 9½″ (21 ×
23.9 cm). Photograph courtesy of The Art Institute of
Chicago (gift of Robert Allerton (1923.944).

C Line has almost unlimited variations.

C

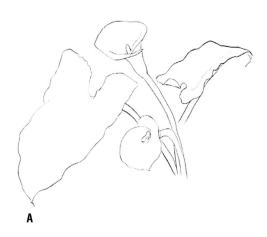

A

B

C

LINE AND SHAPE

Line is important to the artist because it can describe shape, and by shape we recognize objects. Example **A** is immediately understood as a picture of a flower. It does not have the dimension or mass of a flower; it does not have the color or texture of a flower; it is not the actual size of a flower. Nevertheless, we recognize a flower. Ellsworth Kelly has shown us, through his economical use of line, those shapes he felt to be most characteristic of the calla lily.

A cliché states that there are no lines in nature. This may be a bit misleading, since there are line-like elements in our natural and manufactured environment. Such things as tree twigs, telephone wires, spider webs, railroad tracks, and tall grass certainly are linear in feeling. What the cliché is addressing is illustrated in **B** and **C**. Example **B** is a line drawing—a drawing of *lines* that are *not* present in a photograph **(C)** or in the original scene. In the photograph, of course, no black line runs around each object. The lines in drawing actually show *edges,* while in the photo **(C)** areas of different value (or color) meet, showing the end of one object and the beginning of another. Line is therefore, an artistic shorthand, useful because, with comparatively few strokes, an artist can describe and identify shapes so that we understand the image.

Line drawings with the lines describing the edges of various forms abound in art; **D** is just one example. The drawing by Dufy, done quickly with a brush, outlines the many items in the artist's studio with free and loose—but descriptive—lines so that we easily understand the whole scene.

A Ellsworth Kelly. *Calla Lily I*. 1984. Lithograph on Rives BFK paper, edition of 30, 30¼ × 39″ (77 × 99 cm). Courtesy of Ellsworth Kelly and Gemini G.E.L.
B Line, as an artistic shorthand, depicts the edges of shapes.
C Areas of different value delineate the various objects in this scene.
D Raoul Dufy. *The Painter's Studio*. Ca. 1942. Brush and ink, 19⅞ × 26″ (50.4 × 66 cm). The Museum of Modern Art, New York (gift of Mr. and Mrs. Peter A. Rubel).

D

TYPES OF LINE

Line has served artists as a basic tool ever since cave dwellers drew with charred sticks on the cave walls. **Actual lines (A)** may vary greatly in weight, character, and other qualities. Two other types of line also figure importantly in pictorial composition.

An **implied line** is created by positioning a series of points so that the eye tends automatically to connect them. The "dotted line" is an example familiar to us all **(B)**. Think also of the "line" waiting for a bus; several figures standing in a row form an implied line.

A **psychic line** is illustrated in **C**. There is no real line, not even intermittent points; yet we *feel* a line, a mental connection between two elements. This usually occurs when something looks or points in a certain direction. Our eyes invariably follow, and a psychic line results.

All three types of line are present in Perugino's painting of the Crucifixion **(D)**. *Actual lines* are formed, for the edges of figures and background objects are clearly delineated. An *implied line* is created at the bottom, where the Virgin's feet, the base of the cross, and St. John's feet are points that connect into a horizontal line **(E)**. This line is picked up in the horizontal shadows of the side panels. *Psychic lines* occur as our eyes follow the direction in which each figure is looking. St. John looks up at Christ, and Christ gazes down at the Virgin; this gives us a distinct feeling of a central triangle. Both St. Jerome and St. Mary Magdalene also look at Christ, forming a second, broader triangle. The purpose of these lines is to unify or visually tie together the various elements. Perugino's painting **(D)** may seem static, perhaps a bit posed and artificial, but it is admirably organized into a clear, coherent pattern.

Artists should always anticipate the movement of the viewer's eye around their compositions. To a large extent they can control this movement, and the various types of lines can be a valuable tool.

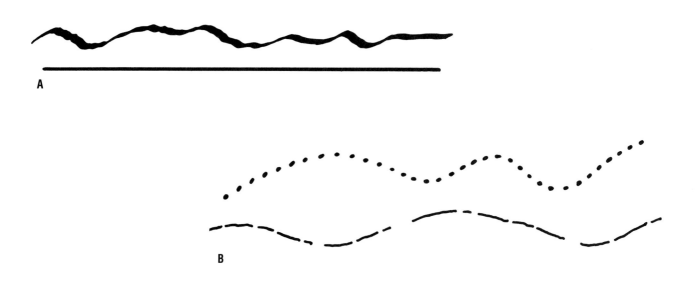

A There are many types of actual lines, each varying in weight and character.

B The points in an implied line are automatically connected by the eye.

C When one object points to another, the eye connects the two in a psychic line.

D Pietro Perugino. *The Crucifixion with the Virgin, St. John, St. Jerome, and St. Mary Magdalene.* Ca. 1485. Oil on panel: center panel 39⅞ × 22¼" (101 × 57 cm); side panels 37½ × 12″ (95 × 31 cm). © 1993 National Gallery of Art, Washington, DC (Andrew W. Mellon Collection).

E Actual, implied, and psychic lines are all present in *The Crucifixion with the Virgin, St. John, St. Jerome, and St. Mary Magdalene.*

D

E

LINE DIRECTION

One important characteristic of line that should be remembered is its *direction*. A horizontal line implies quiet and repose, probably because we associate a horizontal body posture with rest or sleep. A vertical line, such as a standing body, has more potential of activity. But the diagonal line most strongly suggests motion. In so many of the active movements of life (skiing, running, swimming, skating) the body is leaning, so we automatically see diagonals as indicating movement. There is no doubt that we imply more action, more dynamic momentum, from **B** than from **A**. Example **A** is a static, calm pattern; **B** is changing and exciting.

One other factor is involved in the quality of line direction. The outside format of the vast majority of drawings, designs, paintings, and so forth is rectangular. Therefore, any horizontal or vertical line within the work is parallel to, and repetitive of, an edge of the format. The horizontal and vertical lines within a design are stabilizing elements that reduce any feeling of movement. The lines in **A** are parallel to the top and bottom, but none of the lines in **B** are.

George Bellows' painting **(C)** is dominated by a diagonal line that begins with the one fighter's leg on the left, and continues through the second fighter's shoulder and arm. Other diagonals within the figures create the dynamism of the fight scene. The diagonal gesture of the referee balances the group of three figures and completes a triangle. The vertical and horizontals of the fight ring stabilize the composition and provide a counterpoint to the action depicted.

The family portrait by Matisse **(D)**, with its wealth of varied decorative patterns, is a very lively painting. The decorative exuberance is contained within a structure of predominately horizontal and vertical lines. The rug and its designs, the fireplace and mantel, the couches, and even the figures themselves show a consistent emphasis on the horizontal and vertical. While this painting does not suggest the kind of dynamic movement of the Bellows **(C)**; it does show that a composition based on verticals and horizontals does not have to be boring!

A Horizontal lines usually imply rest or lack of motion.
B Diagonal lines usually imply movement and action.
C George Bellows. *Stag at Sharkey's.* 1909. Oil on canvas, 36 × 48″ (92 × 122.6 cm). © The Cleveland Museum of Art (Hinman B. Hurlbut Collection, 1133.22).
D Henri Matisse. *The Painter's Family.* 1911. Oil on canvas, 4′8½″ × 6′4¾″ (1.43 × 1.94 m). Hermitage, Leningrad.

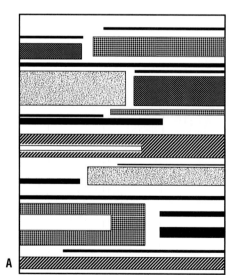

A

B

C

D

A

B

A Jean Auguste Dominique Ingres. *Portrait of Mme Hayard and Her Daughter Caroline*. 1815. Graphite on white wove paper, 11½ × 8⅝″ (292 × 220 cm). Courtesy of The Fogg Art Museum, Harvard University (bequest of Grenville L. Winthrop).

B Alberto Giacometti. *Self-Portrait*. 1954. Pencil, 16 × 12″ (40.5 × 31 cm).

C Rembrandt. *Christ Carrying the Cross*. Ca. 1635. Pen and ink with wash, 5⅝ × 10⅛″ (14 × 26 cm). Kupferstichkabinett, Staatliche Museen, Berlin.

D Deborah Butterfield. *Tango*. 1987. Steel, 28½ × 42 × 15″ (72 × 107 × 38 cm). Edward Thorp Gallery, New York.

C

CONTOUR AND GESTURE

Regardless of the chosen medium, when line is the main element of an image, the result is called a **drawing.** There are two general types of drawings: **contour** and **gesture.**

When line is used to follow the edges of forms, to describe their outlines, the result is called a contour drawing. This is probably the most common use of line in art; **A** is an example. This portrait by Ingres is a precise drawing with extremely delicate lines carefully describing the features and the folds of the clothing. The slightly darker emphasis of the head establishes the focal point. We cannot help but admire the sureness of the drawing, the absolute accuracy of observation.

The self-portrait by Giacometti **(B)** is not composed of the precise contours we find in **A**. Instead, we see many lines which taken together suggest the mass and volume of the head. The result is more active, and we can more readily observe the artist's process of looking and recording. Many of Giacometti's lines follow the topography of the head and find surface contours *within* the form of the head, not merely at the outer edge.

The other common type of drawing is called a gesture drawing. In this instance, describing shapes is less important than showing the action taking place. Line does not stay at the edges, but moves freely within forms. Gesture drawings are not drawings of objects so much as drawings of movement. Because of its very nature, this type of drawing is almost always created quickly and spontaneously. It captures the momentary changing aspect of the subject, rather than recording nuances of form. Rembrandt's *Christ Carrying the Cross* **(C)** is a gesture drawing. Some quickly drawn lines suggest the contours, but most of the lines are concerned with the action of the falling, moving figures.

Deborah Butterfield's *Tango* **(D)** is a sculpture that conveys a sense of drawing in three dimensions. The found objects and steel scraps suggest the presence of a horse with almost "scribble-like" lines. These lines largely define the horse from the inside of the form and the gesture of the pose. Butterfield's work has a spontaneous appearance we would more likely associate with brush and ink than welded steel.

While quite different approaches to drawing, the two categories of contour and gesture are not mutually exclusive. Many drawings combine elements of both, as can be seen in Giacometti's *Self-Portrait* **(B)**. And, as is the case with **D**, the elements of contour or gestural line can also be found in artworks other than traditional drawing.

D

LINE QUALITY

To state that an artist uses line is not very descriptive, because line is capable of infinite variety. The illustrations on these two pages give only a sampling of the linear possibilities available to the artist.

Example **A** shows a drawing by Ingres. Like many drawings, this was a study for a later painting, the *Grande Odalisque*. Artists often use the relatively easy and quick medium of drawing to try various compositional possibilities. Drawing **A** is an extremely elegant image. The sinuous, flowing curves of the nude are rendered in a delicate, restrained, light, often almost disappearing line. The actual proportions of the body are altered to stress the long, sweeping, opposing curves that give the drawing its feeling of quiet grace.

The untitled drawing by Susan Rothenberg shown in **B** is characterized by heavy, blunt contours echoed by thinner coarse lines. The brutal line quality which describes dismembered horse shapes is as appropriate to the imagery as Ingres' lines are to his graceful figure.

The drawing by Daumier **(C)** takes advantage of a variety in line quality from bold to light. The heavier lines bring attention to the figure on the far right, who literally wags his finger at the surprised lawyer. Elsewhere in the drawing lighter lines dissolve into the page, suggesting figures out of focus in the background.

The linear technique you choose can produce emotional or expressive qualities in the final pattern. Solid and bold, quiet and flowing, delicate and dainty, jagged and nervous, or countless other possibilities will influence the effect on the viewer of your drawing or design. Choose a theme or decide the effect you wish to impart, and fit the linear technique to it.

A Jean Auguste Dominique Ingres. Study for the *Grande Odalisque*. Ca. 1814. Pencil, 4⅞ × 10½″ (12 × 27 cm). Musée du Louvre, Paris.
B Susan Rothenberg. *Untitled*. 1978. Acrylic, flashe, pencil on paper, 20 × 20″ (51 × 51 cm). Collection Walker Art Center, Minneapolis (Art Center Acquisition Fund, 1979).
C Honoré Daumier. *The Criminal Case*. N.d. Pen and ink and black chalk, 7⅛ × 11¼″ (18 × 29 cm). Victoria and Albert Museum, London. Crown Copyright.

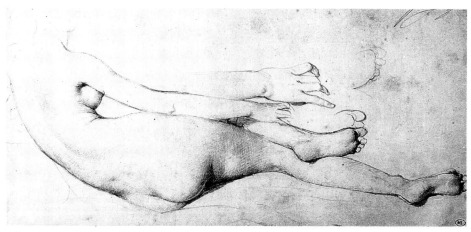

A

B

C

A

B

LINE AS VALUE

A single line can show the shape of objects. But an outlined shape is essentially flat; it does not suggest the volume of the original subject.

The artist can, by placing a series of lines close together, create visual areas of gray. By varying the number of lines and their proximity, an almost limitless number of "grays" can be produced. These resulting areas of dark and light (called areas of **value**) can begin to give the three-dimensional quality lacking in a pure contour line. Again, the specific linear technique and the quality of line can vary a great deal among different artists.

The pen-and-ink image of Eve **(A)**—a detail from Dürer's *Adam and Eve*—shows a strong contour edge because the light body contrasts with a stark brown background. Within the figure Dürer then added parallel lines in a crisscross pattern (called **cross-hatching**) to create areas of gray, which give roundness to the figure. The pen produced necessarily hard, definite strokes, which Dürer carefully controlled in direction to follow the volumes of body forms.

The same pen-and-ink cross-hatching technique is clear in **B**. But in this illustration, the artist, Brad Holland, has used the lines in a looser manner, and the areas of gray are now more important and dominant than the outside contours.

Both **A** and **B** use line to create carefully naturalistic volumes and shapes. In the drawing by Henry Moore **(C)**, the linear technique is very loose, more spontaneous, and quickly scribbled. The volumes of the figure are now more suggested than carefully delineated. The medium is the same, but the technique is different.

The linocut portrait in **D** uses white lines on black to create areas of bold, crisp patterns. While the various values of gray created relate to the planes of the face, it is in an abstract, schematic manner, and the effect is highly decorative. It is a contrast to the precise exactitude of trying to reproduce appearance found in **A**.

D

C

A

B

C

LINE IN PAINTING

Line can be an important element in painting. Since painting basically deals with areas of color, its effect is different from that of drawing, which limits the elements involved. Line becomes important to painting when the artist purposely chooses to outline forms, as Alice Neel does in her portrait **(A)**. Dark lines define the edges of the figure, the chair, and the large plant. The lines are bold and quite obvious.

Line can be seen in the detail of Venus from Botticelli's famous painting **(B)**. The goddess' hair is a beautiful pattern of flowing, graceful, swirling lines. The hand is delineated from the breast by only the slightest value difference; a dark, now quite delicate line clearly outlines the hand.

Compare the use of line in Botticelli's painting with that in **C**. Both works stress the use of line, but the similarity ends there. *Nurse*, by Roy Lichtenstein **(C)**, employs an extremely heavy, bold line—almost a crude line reminiscent of the drawing in comic books. Each artist has adapted his technique to his theme. Compare the treatment of the hair. Venus **(B)** is portrayed as the embodiment of all grace and beauty, her hair a mass of elegant lines in a delicate arabesque pattern. The nurse's hair **(C)**, by contrast, is a flat, colored area boldly outlined, with a few slashing, heavy strokes to define its texture. In a comment on North American culture, aesthetics and subtlety have been stripped away, leaving a crass, blatantly commercial image.

The use of a black or dark line in a design is often belittled as a ''crutch.'' There is no doubt that a dark linear structure can often lend desirable emphasis when the initial color or value pattern seems to provide little excitement. Many artists, both past and present, have purposely chosen to exploit the decorative quality of dark line to enhance their work **(D)**.

A Alice Neel. *Nancy and the Rubber Plant.* 1975. Oil on canvas, 6′8″ × 3′ (2.03 × 0.91 m). Courtesy of the artist.

B Sandro Botticelli. *The Birth of Venus*, detail. Ca. 1480. Oil on canvas; entire work: 5′8⅞″ × 9′1⅞″ (1.75 × 2.79 m). Galleria degli Uffizi, Florence.

C Roy Lichtenstein. *Nurse.* 1964. Magna on canvas, 4′ (1.22 m) square. © Roy Lichtenstein.

D Fernand Léger. *Homage to Louis David.* 1948–49. Oil on canvas, 60½ × 72¾″ (153.7 × 184.8 cm). Musée National d'Art Moderne de la Ville de Paris.

D

A

B

A Jacques Louis David. *The Death of Socrates*. 1787.
Oil on canvas, 4′3″ × 6′5¼″ (1.3 × 1.96 m).
Metropolitan Museum of Art, New York (Wolfe
Fund, 1931. Catharine Lorillard Wolfe Collection,
31.35).

B Juan Gris. *Guitar and Flowers*. 1912. Oil on canvas,
44⅛ × 27⅝″ (112 × 70 cm). The Museum of
Modern Art, New York (bequest of Anna Erickson
Levene in memory of her husband, Dr. Phoebus
Aaron Theodor Levene).

C Berthe Morisot. *In the Dining Room*. 1886. Oil on
canvas, 24⅛ × 19¾″ (61.3 × 50 cm). © 1993
National Gallery of Art, Washington, DC (Chester
Dale Collection).

D Brice Marden. *Cold Mountain 6 (Bridge)*. 1988–91.
Oil on linen, 108 × 144″ (2.7 × 3.7 m). Courtesy
Mary Boone Gallery, New York.

C

LINE IN PAINTING

Line becomes important in a painting when the contours of the forms are sharply defined, and the viewer's eye is drawn to the edges of the various shapes. David's painting *The Death of Socrates* **(A)** contains no actual outlines, as we have seen in other examples. However, the contour edges of the many figures are very clearly defined. A clean edge separates each of the elements in the painting, so that a line tracing of these edges would show us the whole scene. The color adds interest, but we are most aware of the essential drawing underneath. As a mundane comparison, remember the coloring books we had as children and, as we took out our crayons, the parental warnings to "stay within the lines." Despite the absence of actual lines, the David work would be classified as a "linear" painting.

A linear painting is distinguished by its clarity. The emphasis on edges, with the resulting separation of forms, makes a clear, definite statement. Even an abstract painting, which simplifies form and ignores details, presents this effect **(B)**.

There are other possible roles that explicit lines can play in painting besides the clear definition of shape or form. Some artists use a linear technique in applying color. The color areas are built up by repeated linear strokes that are not smoothed over. *In the Dining Room* **(C)** by Berthe Morisot is an example of this technique, which was employed by many artists of the Impressionist period.

Brice Marden paints with a brush, the handle of which is often lengthened to amplify the gesture of his stroke. *Cold Mountain 6* **(D)** is composed of repeated linear strokes that create a complex pattern. The lines are calligraphic in nature, suggesting the flow of writing. Even the apparently casual drips are linear elements in the rhythmic structure of this painting.

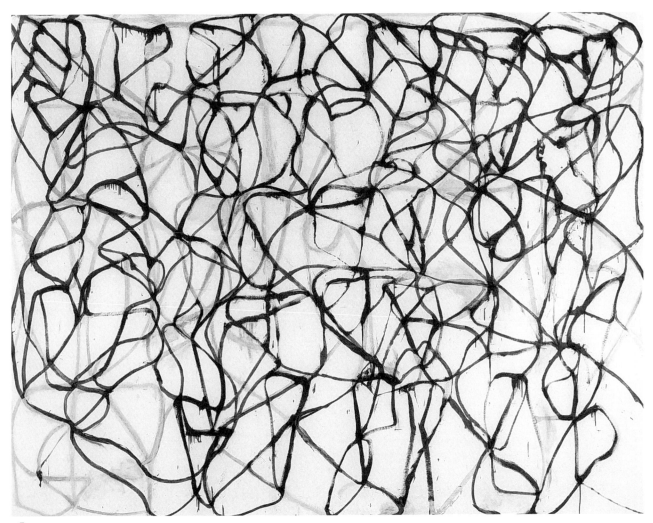

D

A

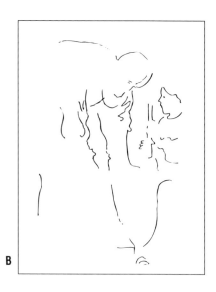

B

A Georges de la Tour. *Joseph the Carpenter*. Ca. 1645.
38½ × 28½″ (98 × 72 cm). Musée du Louvre, Paris.

B A line drawing of *Joseph the Carpenter* is confusing
because the shapes are defined by changing light and
shadow, not by line.

C Sophie Taeuber-Arp. *Parasols*. 1938. Painted wood
relief, 34 × 24″ (86 × 61 cm). Rijksmuseum Kröller-
Müller, Otterlo.

D Sophie Taeuber-Arp. *Untitled* (Study for Parasols).
1937. Black crayon, 13½ × 10″ (34 × 25 cm).
Foundation Jean Arp and Sophie Taeuber-Arp,
Rolandseck, Germany.

E Mark Feldstein. *Untitled (from Unseen New York)*.
1975. Gelatin silver print, 14 × 11″ (35 × 28 cm).
© Mark Feldstein, 1975.

C

D

LOST-AND-FOUND CONTOUR

Joseph the Carpenter **(A)** is a painting by Georges de la Tour which puts more emphasis on color and value than on line. In each of the figures, only part of the body is revealed by a sharp contour, but the edge then disappears into a mysterious darkness. This is termed **lost-and-found contour:** Now you see it, now you don't. The artist gives us a few clues, and we fill in the rest. For example, when we see a sharply defined hand, we will automatically assume an arm is there, although we do not see it. A line interpretation **(B)** of this painting proves that we do not get a complete scene, but merely suggestions of form. Bits and pieces float, and it is more difficult to understand the image presented.

A strong linear contour structure in a painting provides clarity. Lost-and-found contour gives only relative clarity, but is in fact closer to our natural perception of things. Seldom do we see everything before us in equal and vivid contrast. The relief shown in **C** presents a rhythmic linear composition created by only those edges cast in shadow. In this case of a ''white-on-white'' relief, it is the illuminated edges that disappear. We can get a better idea of the ''lost'' contours from the study drawing shown in **D**. Obviously a different composition of lines in **C** would be revealed with a change in the direction of light.

Photographers often choose the lighting for a subject to exploit the emotional and expressive effects of lost-and-found contour. Example **E** is just one of the countless photographs that have used the technique. Here a very beautiful and dramatic image has been produced from a simple architectural detail.

E

8

SHAPE
VOLUME

A

A Judith Leyster. *Still Life*. 17th century. Oil on canvas, 26¾ × 24⅜″ (68 × 62 cm). Fine Arts Mutual, Inc., London.

B J. M. W. Turner. *Music Party, East Cowes Castle*. Ca. 1835. Oil on canvas, 40 × 30 feet (1213 × 905 cm). Clore Collection, Tate Gallery, London.

C Spatially organized image of Abraham Lincoln. Blocpix® image from photograph by Matthew Brady. Courtesy E. T. Manning.

B

INTRODUCTION

A **shape** is a visually perceived area created either by an enclosing line or by color and value changes defining the outer edges. A shape can also be called a **form.** These two terms are generally synonymous and are often used interchangeably. Shape is a more precise term because form has other meanings in art. For example, form may be used in a broad sense to describe the total visual organization of a work. A work's "artistic form" refers not just to shape but also to color, texture, value pattern, composition, and balance. Thus, to avoid confusion, the term *shape* is more specific.

Design, or composition, is basically the arrangement of shapes. The still life painted by seventeenth-century artist Judith Leyster **(A)** is an arrangement of various circular shapes varying in size. Of course, the color, texture, and value of these shapes are important, but the basic element is shape. Pictures certainly exist without color, without any significant textural interest, and even without line—but rarely without shape. Only the fuzziest, most diffuse atmospheric images of light **(B)** can be said almost to dispense with shape.

In designing your own patterns and looking at others' patterns, you must develop the ability to look beyond interesting subject matter to the basic element of shape. The circles in **A** literally represent a basket, a glass, a jug, and various fruits. In another picture, the circle could be a wheel, the sun, an angel's halo, or some other round item. However, the circle's importance in pictorial composition is as a *shape.* In design, seeing shapes is primary; reading their meaning is interesting, but secondary.

Example **C** is a picture created by a computer. The image is interesting because it is clearly a pattern of some 250 squares of various grays and, incidentally, is a picture of Abraham Lincoln. In **C** a midpoint has been established at which we are aware equally of the basic design shapes and the subject matter. Several images were tested to find this midpoint in which most people could see both qualities. When fewer, larger squares were used, people saw only the gray shapes and not Lincoln's head.

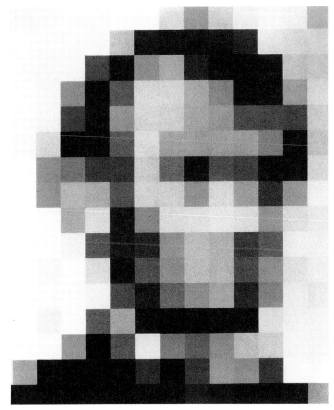

C

VOLUME/MASS

Shape usually is considered a two-dimensional element, and the words **volume,** or **mass,** are applied to the three-dimensional equivalent. In simplest terms, paintings have shapes and sculptures have masses. The same terms and distinctions that are applied to shapes apply to three-dimensional volumes or masses. Although the two concepts are closely related, the design considerations of the artist can differ considerably when working in a two- or three-dimensional medium.

A flat work, such as a painting, can be viewed satisfactorily only from a limited number of angles and offers approximately the same image from each angle, but three-dimensional works can be viewed from countless angles as we move around them. The three-dimensional design changes each time we move; the forms are constantly seen in differing relationships. Unless we purposely stop and stare at a piece of sculpture, our visual experience is always fluid, not static. The two photographs of the piece of sculpture by David Smith **(A)** show how radically the design pattern can change depending on our angle of perception.

Thus, in composing art of three-dimensional volume or mass, the artist has more complex considerations. We may simply step back to view the progress of our painting or drawing. With sculpture, we must view the work from a multitude of angles, anticipating all the viewpoints from which it may be seen.

Architecture is the art form most concerned with three-dimensional volumes. Unlike painting or drawing, architecture does not reproduce pictures or models of existing natural objects, but creates three-dimensional shapes by enclosing areas within walls.

A sharp, clear-cut label for art as either two- or three-dimensional is not always possible. Relief sculptures are three-dimensional, but because the carving is relatively shallow with a flat back, they actually function more as paintings without color. And many contemporary artists now incorporate three-dimensional elements by attaching items to the canvas, or presenting them with the canvas. In the work by Jennifer Bartlett **(B)** a painting of boats is juxtaposed against three-dimensional versions of the same image. These sculptural elements refer more to the shapes in the painting than to real boats. They are cropped at the same points as the images are cropped in the painting. In this case, the three-dimensional form seems to copy the painting, rather than the usual idea of the painting following the appearance of the three-dimensional form.

Many artists today attempt to break down the dividing barriers between painting, sculpture, architecture, and even theater. In such cases the content determines the appropriate forms. Malcolm Cochran's *Western Movie* **(C)** includes a wide-screen projection of a nineteenth-century painting of Niagara Falls. Moving images of water are projected on top of this from several film projectors. The area in front of the large curved screen is occupied by amusement-ride horses which are moving up and down. The whole **installation** is presented in a gallery space transformed into a theater-like setting. This complex artwork evokes ideas of the American frontier through a variety of media, and incorporates the element of time as well.

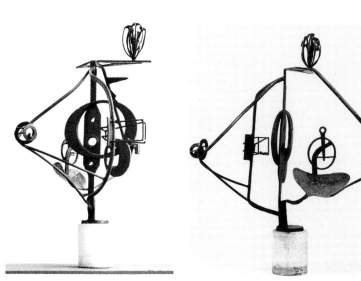

A David Smith. *Blackburn: Song of an Irish Blacksmith,* front and side views, 1949–50. Steel and bronze, 46¼ × 41 × 24″ (117 × 104 × 61 cm); height of base 8″ (20 cm), diameter 7¼″ (18 cm). Wilhelm Lehmbruck Museum, Duisburg, Germany.

B Jennifer Bartlett. *Boats.* 1987. Sculpture: painted wood, steel support, pine mast, 66½ × 47½ × 46″ each (169 × 121 × 117 cm); painting: oil on canvas, 9′10″ × 14′ (3 × 4.3 m). Courtesy Paula Cooper Gallery, New York.

C Malcolm Cochran. *Western Movie.* 1990. Installation.

A

B

C

NATURALISM AND DISTORTION

The magazine cover in **A** shows the difference of the two terms **naturalism** and **distortion.** By a clever adaptation of two well-known paintings, we can see the contrast. The right-hand woman (from a Sargent painting) would be described as *naturalistic.* The artist has skillfully reproduced the visual image, the forms, and the proportions seen in nature, with an illusion of volume and three-dimensional space. Naturalism is what most people call ''realism,'' meaning, of course, *visual* realism. On the left side, there is another woman (from a Picasso painting) shown in what is called *distortion.* In using distortion, the artist disregards the shapes and forms of nature, purposely changing or exaggerating them. Sometimes distortion is meant to provoke an emotional response on the part of the viewer; sometimes it serves merely to emphasize the design elements inherent in the subject matter.

Many people think that distortion is a twentieth-century development. Now that the camera can easily and cheaply re-produce the appearance of the world around us—a role formerly filled by painting—distortion or its degree has greatly increased in twentieth-century art. However, distortion has always been a facet of art; the artist has rarely been merely a human camera. Distortion of the figures is clear in the four-teenth-century wooden statue in **B**. The subject is Mary holding the body of the crucified Christ. The greatly exaggerated distortion of usual body proportions emphasizes the agony of the theme.

In **C** the contemporary French sculptor Germaine Richier uses even greater distortion of human shapes and proportions. The grossly elongated forms and sharply acute angles of the limbs take on the attributes of the insect that the title suggests. The lumpy, uneven surface in **C** is a further distortion of the human body. This purposeful disregard of the naturalistic image achieves an emotional and quite menacing image.

A

B

A Cover drawing by Russell Connor, November 23,
   1992; © 1992 The New Yorker Magazine, Inc.
B Röttgen Pieta. Ca. 1370. Wood, 10½″ (27 cm) high.
   Rheinisches Landesmuseum, Bonn.
C Germaine Richier. *Praying Mantis*. N.d. Bronze.
   Height 4′5″ (1.35 m). Courtesy John Cowles Family.

C

NATURALISM AND IDEALISM

Naturalism is concerned with *appearance*. It gives the true-to-life, honest visual appearance of shapes in the world around us. In contrast, there is a specific type of artistic distortion called **idealism**. Idealism reproduces the world not as it is but as it should be. Nature is improved upon. All the flaws, accidents, and incongruities of the visual world are corrected.

The self-portrait by Gregory Gillespie **(A)** is naturalistic. Even in painting himself, the artist has indulged in no flattery. If anything, perhaps he has chosen to emphasize the imperfect. The fifth-century B.C. statue **(B)** illustrates the opposite approach—idealism. This statue was a conscious attempt to discover the ideal proportions of the human body. No human figure was copied for this sculpture. The statue represents a visual paragon, a conceptual image of perfection that nature simply does not produce.

Idealism is a recurrent theme in art, as it is in civilized society. We are all idealistic; we all strive for perfection. Despite overwhelming historical evidence, we continue to believe we can create a world without war, poverty, sickness, or social injustice. Obviously, art will periodically reflect this dream of a utopia.

Today we are all familiar with a prevalent, if mundane, form of idealism. Large numbers of the advertisements we see daily are basically idealistic. Beautiful people in romantically lit, luxurious settings induce an atmosphere that is far different from the daily lives of most of us. But yet we do enjoy the glimpse of the ''never-never land'' awaiting if we use a certain product. Governments also often employ idealistic images to convince the world (or themselves) that their particular political system is superior. The heroic, triumphant figures in **C** are an example. Political propaganda is generally only naturalistic when portraying the opponent.

A

A Gregory Gillespie. *Myself Painting a Self Portrait.*
1980–81. Mixed media on wood, 4′10⅛″ × 5′8¾″
(1.48 × 1.75 m). Hirshhorn Museum and Sculpture
Garden, Smithsonian Institution (museum purchase
with funds donated by the Board of Trustees, 1981).

B Polyclitus. *Doryphorus (Spear Bearer).* Roman copy
after Greek original of Ca. 450–440 B.C. Marble,
height 6′6″ (1.98 m). Museo Nazionale, Naples.

C Vera Mukhina. *Machine Tractor Driver and
Collective Farm Girl.* N.d. Sculpture, U.S.S.R.
Economic Achievement Exhibition, Moscow.

B

C

ABSTRACTION

A specific kind of artistic distortion is called **abstraction.** Abstraction implies a simplification of natural shapes to their essential, basic character. Details are ignored as the shapes are reduced to their simplest terms. The computer-assisted illustration in **A** is an example of abstraction.

Since no artist, no matter how skilled or careful, can possibly reproduce every detail of a natural subject, any painting could be called an abstraction. But the term *abstraction* is most often applied to works in which simplification is visually obvious and important to the final pictorial effect. Of course, the degree of abstraction can vary. In **A**, almost all the elements have been abstracted to some extent. Many details have been omitted in reducing the camera and figure to basic geometric shapes (primarily circles and squares). Still, the subject matter is immediately recognizable, and we are not too far from the naturalistic image. When the degree of abstraction is slight, as in this example, we often consider the shapes to be generalized or stylized.

Abstraction is not a new technique; artists have employed this device for centuries. If anything, the desire for naturalism in art is the more recent development. The Eskimo ceremonial carving in **B** clearly shows abstracted forms. Although the result is quite different from **A**, many of the shapes in this mask also seem to suggest geometric forms. This illustrates the widely accepted principle: All form, however complex, is essentially based on, and can be reduced to, a few geometric shapes.

Not all abstraction necessarily results in a geometric conclusion. And abstraction can result in imagery that is not as directly derived from natural references as the previous examples. The simple petal-like shapes in Arshile Gorky's *Garden in Sochi* (**C**) suggest plants, and even human anatomy, without explicitly resembling anything nameable. Abstract shapes such as these, which allude to natural, organic forms, are called **biomorphic.**

A

A *Press Photographer*. 1991. Exhibit Marketing, Design firm; Scott Goldman, Ron Chan, Designers; Ron Chan, Illustrator.

B Mask of *Tunghak, Keeper of the Game.* Inuit (south of the lower Yukon). 19th century. Painted wood, width 36¼″ (93 cm). National Museum of Natural History, Smithsonian Institution.

C Arshile Gorky. *Garden in Sochi.* Ca. 1943. Oil on canvas, 31 × 39″ (79 × 99 cm). The Museum of Modern Art, New York (acquired through the Lillie P. Bliss Bequest).

B

C

A

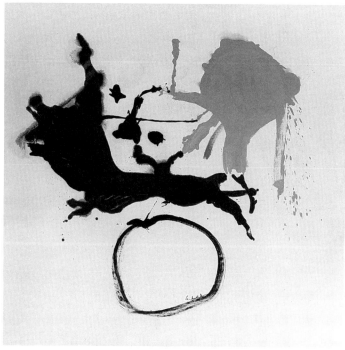

B

A Lyubov Popova. *Embroidery design for Verbovka.* 1917. Collage on gray cardboard, 3⅜ × 6½″ (8.7 × 16.5 cm). Private collection, Moscow.

B Helen Frankenthaler. *Over the Circle.* 1961. Oil on canvas, 84 × 87″ (213 × 221 cm). Archer M. Huntington Art Gallery, The University of Texas at Austin (gift of Mari and James A. Michener, 1991).

C Tony Smith. *Gracehoper.* 1961. Welded steel and paint, 23 × 22 × 46′ (7.01 × 6.71 × 14.02 m). © The Detroit Institute of Arts (Founders Society purchase, donations from W. Hawkins Ferry, Mr. and Mrs. Walter Buhl Ford II Fund, Eleanor Clay Ford, Marie and Alex Manoogian Funds, and members of the Friends of Modern Art).

NONOBJECTIVE SHAPES

According to common usage, the term *abstraction* might be applied to the painting in **A**. This would be misleading, however, because the shapes in this work are not natural forms that have been artistically simplified. They do not represent anything other than the geometric forms we see. Rather, they are pure forms. A better term to describe these shapes is **nonobjective**—that is, shapes with no object reference and non subject-matter suggestion.

Most of the original design drawings in this book are nonobjective patterns. Often, it is easier to see an artistic principle or element without a distracting veneer of subject matter. In a similar way, many artists in this century are forcing us to observe their works as visual patterns, not story-telling narratives. Without a story, subject, or even definable shapes, a painting must be appreciated solely as a visual design. Lack of subject matter does not necessarily eliminate emotional content in the image. Some nonobjective works are cool, aloof, and unemotional. Paintings such as **A** present purely nonobjective, geometric shapes that are, as Plato said,'' free from the sting of desire.'' Example **B** is equally nonobjective, but the shapes are not geometric and seem to have developed from the inherently fluid quality of the paint. The canvas seems to be a record of the paint flowing and pooling under the artist's direction.

Whether any shape can be truly nonobjective is a good question. Can we really look at a circle just as a *circle* without beginning to think of some of the countless round objects in our environment? Artists often make use of this instinctive human reflex. A work such as Tony Smith's sculpture **(C)** appears to be a totally nonobjective pattern of forms, yet it reminds us of something. Reading the title *Gracehoper* immediately transforms the image into shapes reminiscent of a giant insect (''grasshopper''). Such reactions, even when not planned, are almost inevitable.

C

RECTILINEAR AND CURVILINEAR

The chairs shown in **A** and **B** illustrate the difference in two terms that are commonly applied to shapes: **rectilinear** and **curvilinear.** Two objects with the same function are visually quite different in design. The Thonet chair **(A)** is constructed using all rounded, curving forms: a *curvilinear* design. The Breuer chair **(B)** is the opposite. Now all the forms have straight edges, giving a sharp, angular feeling. *Rectilinear* is the term to describe this visual effect.

The painting by Theo van Doesburg **(C)** is clearly a rectilinear design. The title describes a theme of card players. However, the forms are so highly abstracted that any subject matter becomes unimportant. What we see is a busy pattern of light and dark shapes that are all geometric in feeling: hard, straight edges of rectangular forms.

The bicycle poster in **D** shows an equal emphasis on the opposite curvilinear type of shape. There is barely a straight line to be found. This poster is a product of a late nineteenth-century style called *Art Nouveau,* which put total pictorial emphasis on curvilinear or natural shapes.

We do think of curvilinear shapes as *natural,* reflecting the soft, flowing shapes found in nature. Rectilinear shapes, being more regular and precise, suggest geometry and, hence, appear more artificial and manufactured. Of course, these are very broad conclusions. In fact, geometric shapes abound in nature, especially in the microscopic structure of elements; and people design many objects with irregular, free-form shapes.

Illustrations **C** and **D** concentrate exclusively on a single type of shape. Most art combines both types. In using the two types of shapes, a useful device is to stress one type and use the other sparingly, as a point of emphasis. In the Gris painting **(E)**, the table and wall panels make a rigid pattern of sharply defined rectilinear shapes, while the curves of the violin break the angular pattern and create a natural focal point.

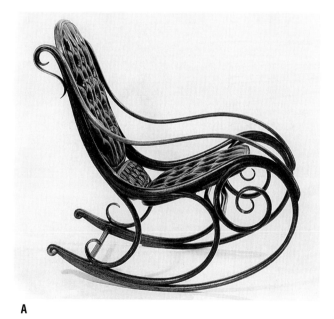

A

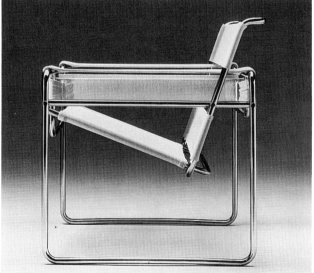

B

C

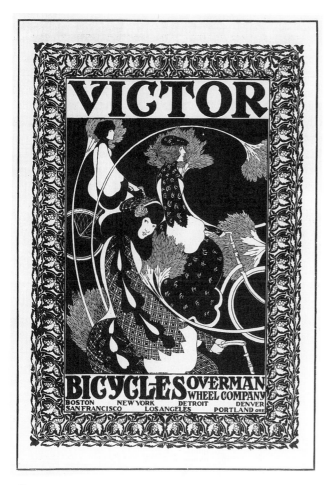

D

E

A Michael Thonet. *Rocking Chair*. Ca. 1860. Bent
mahoganized beechwood upholstered in black leather.
The Brooklyn Museum (Caroline A. L. Pratt Fund,
69.79.1).

B Marcel Breuer. *Wassily Chair*, 1925. Seamless
tubular steel with polished chrome finish and leather,
31″ (79 cm) wide × 27½″ (70 cm) deep × 28¾″ (73
cm) high. Wassily Chair, Knoll Studio, The Knoll
Group.

C Theo van Doesburg. *Composition IX, Opus 18 (Card
Players)*. 1917. Oil on canvas, 45¼ × 41⅜″ (116 ×
106 cm). Gemeentemuseum, The Hague.

D Will H. Bradley. Poster for Victor Bicycles,
Overman Wheel Company. 1896. Library of
Congress.

E Juan Gris. *The Violin*. 1916. Oil on wood panel,
45½ × 28½″ (117 × 73 cm). Öffentliche
Kunstsammlung Basel, Kunstmuseum.

POSITIVE/NEGATIVE SHAPES

The four examples in **A** illustrate an important design consideration that is sometimes overlooked. In each of these patterns, the black shape is identical. The very different visual effects are caused solely by its placement within the format. This is because the location of the black shape immediately organizes the empty space into various shapes. We often refer to these as **positive** and **negative shapes.** The black shape is a positive element, the white empty space the negative shape or shapes. **Figure** and **ground** are other terms used to describe the same idea—the black shape being the figure.

In paintings with subject matter, the distinction of object and background is usually clear. It is important to remember that both elements have been thoughtfully designed and planned by the artist. The subject is the focal point, but the negative areas created are equally important in the final pictorial effect. Japanese art often intrigues the Western viewer because of its unusual design of the negative spaces. In the Japanese print **(B)** the unusual bend of the central figure and the flow of the robes to touch the edges of the picture create varied and interesting negative spaces. A more usual vertical pose for this figure would have formed more regular, symmetrical shapes in the negative areas.

Negative spaces need not be empty flat areas, as the painting **C** by Mondrian, illustrates. The areas between the branches have brushstrokes as evident and active as those that define the tree. Mondrian attracts our attention to the negative areas with his brushwork, and makes these shapes as much the subject of the painting as the form of the tree. The tree and the surrounding space seem to have been considered as a totality, not as separate elements.

The same positive/negative concept is applicable also to three-dimensional art forms. The sculpture of Henry Moore is noted for the careful integration of negative space "holes" within the composition. Architecture is, in essence, the enclosure of negative spaces. The contrast of positive and negative areas may also be a primary consideration in the overall design, as the house by Michael Graves **(D)** shows.

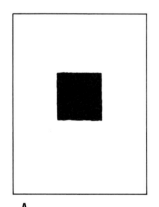 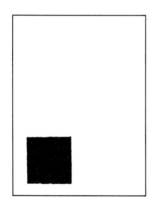  

A

A The location of shapes in space organizes the space into positive and negative areas.
B Tōshūsai Sharaku. *The Actor Segawa Tomisaburō as the Courtesan Toyama Sheltering Ichikawa Kurizō as Higashiyama Yoshiwaka-Maru.* 1794. Woodcut, 13 × 5⅞" (33 × 15 cm). Metropolitan Museum of Art, New York (Elisha Whittelsey Collection, Whittelsey Fund, 1949; JP 3121).
C Piet Mondrian. *The Gray Tree.* 1912. Oil on canvas, 30⅞ × 42½" (78 × 108 cm). Gemeentemuseum, The Hague.
D Michael Graves. Addition to the Benacerraf House. Princeton, New Jersey, 1969.

B

C

D

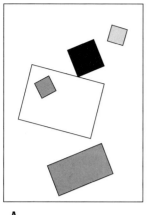

A

B

C

D

A When positive and negative spaces are too rigidly defined, the result can be rather uninteresting.

B If the negative areas are made more interesting, the positive-negative integration improves.

C Georges Seurat. *Silhouette of a Woman*. 1882–84. Conté crayon on paper, 12 × 8⅞″ (30.5 × 22.5 cm). McNay Art Museum, San Antonio, Texas (bequest of Marion Koogler McNay).

D Georges Seurat. *The Black Bow*. Ca. 1882. Conté crayon, 12³⁄₁₆ × 9⅛″ (31 × 32 cm). Musée d'Orsay, Paris.

E Georges Seurat. *The Artist's Mother (Woman Sewing)*. Conté crayon on paper, 12¼ × 9½″ (31 × 24 cm). Metropolitan Museum of Art, New York (Purchase, Joseph Pulitzer Bequest, 55.21.1).

POSITIVE/NEGATIVE SHAPES

INTEGRATION

Design themes and purposes vary, but some integration between positive and negative shapes is generally thought desirable. In **A** the shapes and their placement are interesting enough, but they seem to float aimlessly within the format. They also have what we call a "pasted-on" look, since there is little back-and-forth visual movement between the positive shapes and the negative white background. An unrelieved silhouette of every shape is usually not the most interesting spatial solution. Example **B** shows similar shapes in the same positions as **A**, but the "background" is now broken into areas of value which lend interest as well as better positive/negative integration. The division into positive and negative is flexible.

Three drawings by Georges Seurat demonstrate three degrees of positive/negative integration. The drawing of the female figure shown in **C** presents the figure as a dark shape against a lighter background. For the most part this is a silhouette; positive and negative (figure and ground) are presented as a simple contrast.

The relationship of positive and negative is more complex in **D**. The left side of the figure is dark against a lighter ground, and the right side of the figure is light against a darker ground. This alternation of dark and light makes us aware of the negative shapes, and they take on a stronger visual interest than in **C**.

The composition of **E** presents the most complex integration of positive and negative shapes of the three Seurat drawings. Here, dark, light, and middle values are present as both figure and ground. There are areas of sharp distinction, such as the edge of the arm against the background, and there are also areas of soft or melting transitions where the eye moves smoothly from foreground, to middleground, to background. The soft boundaries of the hair melt into the surrounding background shapes.

The range of positive/negative integration can be found in abstract or nonobjective artworks, as well as in representational images. The shapes in **E** work both as representations (head and wall for example), and as an abstract composition of light and dark shapes.

E

POSITIVE/NEGATIVE SHAPES

CONFUSION

Sometimes positive and negative shapes are integrated to such an extent that there is truly no visual distinction. When we look at the painting in **A**, we automatically see some black shapes on a background. But when we read the artist's title, *White Forms,* suddenly the view changes, and we begin to focus on the *white* shapes, with the black areas now perceived as negative space. The artist has purposely made the positive/negative relationship ambiguous.

The theater poster in **B** has this same quality, as our eyes must shift back and forth from dark to light in seeking the positive element. The first thing we see is a black head in silhouette against a white shape. Then we notice this white area is an outline map of Africa, a map that in the lower right subtly changes and becomes the profile of a young white man. For a play dealing with race relations in South Africa, this design presents both the theme and an intriguing visual pattern.

In most paintings of the past, the separation of object and background was easily seen, even if selected areas merged visually. But several twentieth-century styles literally do away with the distinction. We can see that the subject matter of the painting in **C** is a figure. Despite the Cubist abstractions of natural forms into geometric planes, we can discern the theme. But it is difficult to determine just which areas are part of the figure and which are background. The artist, Picasso, also broke up the "space" in the same Cubist manner. There is no clear delineation of the positive from the negative.

An integration of positive and negative shapes is a feature of many trademark designs and can give an unusual interest to quite simple forms. But the skill of using such complicated forms as cattle heads **(D)** makes this an exceptional design.

A Franz Kline. *White Forms.* 1955. Oil on canvas, 6'2⅜" × 4'2¼" (1.89 × 1.28 m). The Museum of Modern Art, New York (gift of Philip Johnson).
B *"Master Harold" . . . and the boys.* 1985. Poster for Department of Theatre Arts, California State University, Los Angeles. David McNutt, Designer; C.S.U. Creative Media Services, Los Angeles.
C Pablo Picasso. *Daniel-Henry Kahnweiler.* 1910. Oil on canvas, 39⅝ × 28⅝" (101 × 73 cm). Photograph courtesy of The Art Institute of Chicago (gift of Mrs. Gilbert W. Chapman, 1948.561).
D Eastern Breeders symbol. Art Director/Designer: Stephen Kalibatas.

A

"MASTER HAROLD"
...and the boys.

The Award Winning Cal State L.A. Department of Theatre Arts Presents
ATHOL FUGARD'S EXPLORATION OF WHITE SHAME AND BLACK DIGNITY

| Special Guest Artist | With Cal State L.A. Students | Directed By |
| BROCK PETERS | CHRIS SPITLER & ANDRE BROOKS | JOANNE GORDON |

NOVEMBER, 1985
AMERICAN COLLEGE THEATRE FESTIVAL XVIII ENTRY
THE CALIFORNIA STATE UNIVERSITY

B

C

EASTERN
BREEDERS
D

9

TEXTURE

A

A Betye Saar. *The Time Inbetween*. 1974. Wooden box
containing photos, illustration, paint, envelope, metal
findings, beads, fan, glove, tape measure, lace,
buttons, coin purse, velvet ribbon, cloth, feathers,
bones; closed dimensions: 3⅜ × 8½ × 11⅝″ (8.6 ×
21.6 × 29.6 cm). San Francisco Museum of Modern
Art (purchase).
B Arthur Erickson. Private home, Vancouver, B.C.

INTRODUCTION

Texture refers to the surface quality of objects. Texture appeals to our sense of touch. Even when we do not actually feel an object, our memory provides a sensory reaction or sensation of touch. In effect, the various light and dark patterns of different textures give visual clues for us to enjoy the textures vicariously. Of course, all objects have some surface quality, even if it is only an unrelieved smooth flatness. The element of texture is illustrated in art when an artist purposely exploits contrasts in surface to provide visual interest.

Many art forms have a basic concern with textures and its visual effects. In most of the craft areas, texture is an important consideration. Ceramics, jewelry, and furniture design often rely heavily on the texture of the materials to enhance the design effect. In weaving and the textile arts, texture is a primary consideration. The interior designer must be sensitive to the visual effects that textural contrasts can achieve.

In sculpture exhibits, ''Do not touch'' signs are a practical (if unhappy) necessity, for so many sculptures appeal to our enjoyment of texture that we almost instinctively want to touch. The smooth translucence of marble, the rough grain of wood, the polish or patina of bronze, the irregular drop of molten solder—each adds a distinctive textural quality.

Betye Saar's *The Time Inbetween* (**A**) contains a variety of textures, and seems to invite us to explore this intimate collection by handling it. Beads, feathers, bone, and velvet provide a variety of tactile sensations. A photocopy of the artist's hand is included, and underscores the primacy of the sense of touch for this artwork.

Architecture today often relies on changes in texture for visual interest. Applied surface decoration has become less important; emphasis is placed on the honest look and ''feel'' of the materials. The design of the house in **B** uses simple rectangular forms in varying textures. The smooth sheen of glass is contrasted with warm, grained wood in flat horizontal and vertical ribbed patterns. Other areas gain further contrast from the rough, uneven texture of natural stone.

Visual distance can be a factor in texture. From a distance, many surfaces appear relatively smooth. The closer we get, the rougher and more varied the surface becomes, and microscopic photographs can reveal textural patterns invisible to the naked eye.

B

TACTILE TEXTURE

There are two categories of artistic texture—*tactile* and *visual*. Architecture and sculpture employing actual material have what is called **tactile texture**—texture that can actually be felt. In painting, the same term describes an uneven paint surface, when an artist uses thick pigment (a technique called **impasto**) so that a rough, three-dimensional paint surface results.

As the need and desire for illusionism in art faded, tactile texture became a more common aspect of painting. Paintings now could look like what they truly were—paint on canvas. Modifying the painting's surface became another option available to the artist. Van Gogh was an early exponent of the actual application of paint as a further expressive element. The detail in **A** shows how short brushstrokes of thick, undiluted paint are used to build up the agitated, swirling patterns of van Gogh's images. The ridges and raised edges of the paint strokes are obvious to the viewer's eye.

The visual movement of paint strokes—often applied with a palette knife or very large brushes—was an important aspect of many Abstract Expressionist paintings. This technique resembled van Gogh's, but the result was even more dynamic because of the more spontaneous irregular strokes made by the artist. The painting in **B** uses an extremely heavy, rich paint surface created by the thick pigment applied directly with a palette knife. The impression of the paint almost reminds us of frosting generously slathered over a cake.

The dividing line between painting and sculpture disappears in many contemporary works when actual items are attached to the painted surface. The effect is seen in **C**. This is indeed a ''mixed media'' piece with visual emphasis on the bizarre feathers.

A Vincent van Gogh. *Portrait of the Artist*, detail. 1888. Oil. Mme. H. Lutjens, Zurich.

B Jean Paul Riopelle. *Vespéral No. 3*. 1958. Oil on canvas, 44¾ × 63½″ (113.7 × 161.5 cm). © The Art Institute of Chicago (Mary and Leigh B. Block acquisitions fund). All rights reserved.

C Bruce Conner. *St. Valentine's Day Massacre/Homage to Errol Flynn*. 1960. Feathers, nylon, glass and paper on wood, 19¼ × 14½ × 3½″ (48.3 × 36.9 × 8.9 cm). San Francisco Museum of Modern Art (gift of Dr. and Mrs. W. William Gardner).

A

B

C

A

A Mary Bauermeister. *Progressions*. 1963. Pebbles and sand on four plywood panels, 51¼ × 47⅜ × 4¾" (130 × 120 × 12 cm). The Museum of Modern Art, New York (Matthew T. Mellon Foundation Fund).

B Anne Ryan. *Untitled, No. 129*. Ca. 1948–54. Collage on paper, 4¾ × 4¼" (12.1 × 10.8 cm). Courtesy Joan T. Washburn Gallery, New York.

C Lee Bontecou. *Untitled*. 1964. Welded steel with canvas, 6′ × 6′8″ × 1′6″ (1.83 × 2.03 × 0.45 m). Honolulu Academy of Arts.

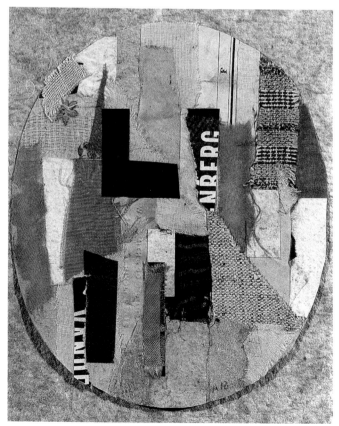

B

TACTILE TEXTURE

COLLAGE

Creating a design by pasting down bits and pieces of colored and textured papers, cloth, or other materials is called **collage.** This artistic technique has been popular for centuries, but mainly in the area of folk art. Only in the twentieth century has collage been seriously considered a legitimate medium of the fine arts.

The collage method is a very serviceable one. It saves the artist the painstaking, often tedious task of carefully reproducing textures in paint. Collage is an excellent medium for beginners. Forms can be altered or reshaped quickly and easily with scissors. Also, compositional arrangements can more easily be tested (before pasting) than when the design is indelibly rendered in paint.

Mary Bauermeister's collage entitled *Progressions* **(A)** is composed of stones and sand on board. Even in the reproduction, one can imagine a range of tactile sensations, from bumpy

to rough. Bauermeister has emphasized the textural qualities of her materials by reducing the composition to a few squares of progressively larger size. Within two of the squares there is also a progression in the size of the pebbles, creating a gradation in texture from fine to coarse. The real physical presence of the materials can be seen in the shadows cast by this collage.

Anne Ryan, an American, worked mainly in collages of cloth. Her untitled collage in **B** shows various bits of cloth in contrasting weaves and textures interspersed with some scraps of printed papers. The dark and light pattern is interesting, but our attention is drawn mainly to the contrast of tactile textures.

Working with old scraps of canvas and welded steel, Lee Bontecou created a textural relief that suggests a series of mouths **(C)**. The inclusion of zippers in several of the open ovals suggests teeth and somehow gives a very frightening appearance to the whole collage.

C

VISUAL TEXTURE

In painting, artists can create the impression of texture on a flat, smooth paint surface. By reproducing the color and value patterns of familiar textures, painters can encourage us to see textures where none actually exist. This is called **visual texture.** The impression of texture is purely visual; it cannot be felt or enjoyed by touch. It is only suggested to our eyes.

One of the pleasures of still-life paintings is the contrast of visual textures. These works, lacking story or emotional content, can be purely visual delights as the artist plays one simulated texture against another. Countless beautiful still-life textures exist from many periods of art. The self-portrait in **A** is by an artist we don't immediately recognize. But the painting is still impressive. The various textures are so beautifully recreated, especially the feathers and the lustrous satin skirt, that we can appreciate the painting for this aspect alone. Many works of the past are still visual pleasures today solely for the artist's ability to render visual texture.

The Surrealist artist Max Ernst uses visual texture to help create the eerie mood of his painting *The Eye of Silence* **(B)**. A dark, stagnant pool is surrounded by rocks and ruins, all encrusted with creeping, decaying vegetation. The convincing rendering of these textures gives the picture its weird, frightening atmosphere.

Visual texture can be an interesting design element even without subject matter or any pictorial reference. The work in **C** is titled *Exploration with a Pencil.* The artist created a composition based solely on areas of contrasting visual textures created with pencil and watercolor.

SEE ALSO: *Value Techniques, page 221.*

A

B

A   Adelaide Labille-Guiard. *Self-Portrait with Two Pupils.* 1785. Oil on canvas, 83 × 59½″ (210.8 × 151.1 cm). The Metropolitan Museum of Art, New York (gift of Julia A. Berwind, 1953.225.5).
B   Max Ernst. *The Eye of Silence.* 1943-1944. Oil on canvas, 3′6½″ × 4′7½″ (1.08 × 1.41 m). Washington University Gallery of Art, St. Louis.
C   Irene Rice Pereira. *Exploration with a Pencil.* 1940. Pencil and gouache, 13⅞ × 17½″ (35 × 44.4 cm). The Museum of Modern Art, New York (gift of Mrs. Marjorie Falk).

C

A

B

C

VISUAL TEXTURE

TROMPE L'OEIL

The ultimate point in portraying visual texture is called **trompe l'oeil,** the French term meaning "to fool the eye." This style is commonly defined as "deceptive painting." In trompe l'oeil, the objects, in sharp focus, are delineated with meticulous care. The artist copies the exact visual color and value pattern of each surface. A deception occurs because the appearance of objects is so skillfully reproduced that we are momentarily fooled. We look closer, even though our rational brain identifies the image as a painting and not the actual object.

It might seem that now, with the camera able to capture easily all the details of appearance, we would have lost our appreciation for this type of painting. But we seem as intrigued as our ancestors in admiring the skill of an artist to produce these effects. The 13-inch-high contemporary painting by Michael Flanagan **(A)** is incredible in the amount of tiny detail the artist has meticulously rendered.

Certainly, twentieth-century artistic emphasis has been on abstractions, distortion, and nonobjective patterns. But in much art the trompe l'oeil tradition continues. In sculpture, the hanging "jacket" **(B)** by Marilyn Levine is incredibly realistic. But it is made of ceramic. The illusion is superb, and we enjoy being visually fooled.

Artists working in this area will often purposely arrange contrasting textures as in **C**. Here a reflecting glass, a rose, a shiny trumpet, and ivory piano keys are arranged in a beautifully rendered composition.

It would also be a mistake to think of trompe l'oeil art as confined to painters with tiny brushes laboring over small-scale easel paintings. More and more today in our cities, we are seeing examples of trompe l'oeil art such as **D**. This "painting" is truly enormous in scale. The entire blank wall of the side of a building has been painted with carefully rendered architectural features and details matching the actual three-dimensional facade.

A Michael Flanagan. *Chalybeate Springs*. 1991. Acrylic, ink and graphite on composition board, 13 × 17″ (33 × 43 cm). Courtesy P.P.O.W., New York.
B Marilyn Levine. *Thom's Jacket*. 1989. Ceramic and mixed media, 34¾ × 23 × 5″ (88 × 58 × 13 cm). O. K. Harris Works of Art, New York.
C Lawrence Walker. *The Horn*. 1993. Mixed media. Vicki Prentice Associates, Inc., Los Angeles.
D Richard Haas. *112 Prince Street Facade*, Prince and Greene Streets, New York. 1974–75. Painted building commissioned by City Walls, Inc. Brooke Alexander, Inc., New York.

D

A

A Printed patterns often serve as decorative elements in interior design.

B Keisai Eisen. *Courtesan in Festive Robes*. Ca. 1830. Color woodcut, 29 × 9¾″ (74 × 25 cm). © The Board of Trustees of the Victoria & Albert Museum, London.

C Gustave Klimt. *Adele Bloch-Bauer*. 1907. Oil on canvas, 44⅝″ (140 cm) square. Österreichische Galerie, Vienna. © Galerie Welz, Salzburg.

B

TEXTURE AND PATTERN

It would be difficult to draw a strict line between *texture* and *pattern*. We immediately associated the word *pattern* with printed fabrics such as plaids, stripes, polka dots, and floral ''patterns'' **(A)**. **Pattern** is usually defined as a repetitive design, with the same motif appearing again and again. **Texture,** too, often repeats, but its variations usually do not involve such perfect regularity. The difference in the two terms is admittedly slight. A material such as burlap would be identified readily as a tactile texture. Yet the surface design is repetitive enough that a photograph of burlap could be called pattern.

The essential distinction between texture and pattern seems to be whether the surface arouses our sense of *touch* or merely provides designs appealing to the eye. In other words,

while every texture makes a sort of pattern, not every pattern could be considered a texture.

In the Japanese woodcut **(B)** there is a wonderful variety of floral and geometric patterns on the figure's kimono. These are simply lovely designs that attract the eye.

The small, intricate designs that dominate the portrait by Klimt in **C** would clearly be called pattern, not texture. While not mechanically repetitive, these designs create decorative colored figures—literally surface patterns—that do not appeal to our sense of touch. The naturalistically rendered body emerging from the ornate, flat, patterned surface provides a startling contrast.

C

10

ILLUSION OF SPACE

INTRODUCTION

Several art forms are three-dimensional and therefore occupy space: ceramics, jewelry and metalwork, weaving, and sculpture, to name a few. In traditional sculpture or in a purely abstract pattern of forms it is important for us to move about and enjoy the changing spatial patterns from various angles. Architecture, of course, is an art form mainly preoccupied with the enclosure of three-dimensional space. A photograph of architecture such as that of the interior court of BCE Place in Toronto **(A)** can only hint at the spectacular feeling of space and volume we experience when actually in the area.

In two-dimensional art forms, such as drawings, paintings, and prints, the artist often wants to convey a feeling of space or depth. Here space is an illusion, for the images rendered on paper, canvas, or board are essentially flat.

This illusion of space is an option for the artist. Painting **B**, by Auguste Herbin, is a dynamic pattern of shapes that remain flat on the **picture plane,** the frontal plane of the painting. Nothing encourages us to see ''back'' into the composition. On the other hand, Gustave Caillebotte's painting **(C)** pierces the picture plane. We are encouraged to forget that a painting is merely a flat piece of canvas. Instead, we are almost standing with the figures in the painting, and our eyes are led to the distant buildings across the bridge. Caillebotte's images suggest three-dimensional forms in a ''real'' space. The picture plane no longer exists as a plane, but becomes a ''window'' into a simulated three-dimensional world created by the artist. A very convincing illusion is created. Many artists, through the centuries, have studied this problem of presenting a visual illusion of space and depth. Several devices have been used.

A

B

A The Galleria, BCE Place, Toronto.
B Auguste Herbin. *Composition on the Word "Vie," 2.*
   1950. Oil on canvas, 57½ × 38¼″ (146 × 97 cm).
   The Museum of Modern Art, New York (The Sidney
   and Harriet Janis Collection).
C Gustave Caillebotte. *Le Pont de l'Europe.* 1876. Oil
   on canvas, 49⅛ × 71⅛″ (124.7 × 180.6 cm). Musée
   du Petit Palais, Geneva.

C

DEVICES TO SHOW DEPTH

SIZE

The easiest way to create an illusion of space or distance is through **size.** Very early in life we observe the visual phenomenon that objects, as they get farther away, appear to become smaller. Thus, when we look at the landscape by Max Beckmann **(A)** we immediately see the relative sizes of the various elements and understand the space that is suggested. The repeating forms of the palm trees gradually diminish in size and effectively lead us back into space along the narrowing lines of the central road. The effect is heightened by the quite large chair back and plant leaves at the bottom of the composition. We forget the innate flatness of a picture, and the picture plane becomes like a window through which we view a three-dimensional scene.

A difference in size to give a feeling of depth is not confined to naturalistic paintings. Saul Steinberg's whimsical lithograph **(B)** uses exactly the same device. Various linear cartoon-like figures and other elements are placed in quite a deep space based on differences in size.

Notice that the size factor can be effective even with abstract shapes, when the forms have no literal meaning or representational quality **(C)**. The smaller squares automatically begin to recede, and we see a spatial pattern.

With abstract figures, the spatial effect is more pronounced if (as in **C**) the same shape is repeated in various sizes. The device is less effective when different shapes are used **(D)**.

A

B

A Max Beckmann. *Landscape, Cannes.* 1934. Oil on canvas, 27⅝ × 39½″ (70 × 100 cm). San Francisco Museum of Modern Art (gift of Louise S. Ackerman).

B Saul Steinberg, *Main Street.* 1973. Lithograph, printed in color, composition: 15¾ × 22″ (40 × 56 cm). The Museum of Modern Art, New York (gift of Celeste Bartos).

C If the same shape is repeated in different sizes, a spatial effect can be achieved.

D With differing shapes, the spatial illusion is not as clear.

D

C

DEVICES TO SHOW DEPTH

SIZE

Using relative sizes to give a feeling of space or depth is very common to many periods and styles of art. Some artists have taken this basic idea and exaggerated it by increasing the size differences. In the Japanese woodcut **(A)** the one fish kite is very large and hence seems quite close. By contrast, the other smaller kites and the tiny figures, trees, and hills seem far in the distance. There are two advantages to this practice. First, seeing a kite drawn larger than human figures automatically forces us to imagine the great distance involved. Second, this very contrast of large and tiny elements can create a dynamic visual pattern.

The circus scene by Demuth **(B)** uses the same idea. One performer is shown very large and hence is in the foreground. The other trapeze artists are shown smaller and recede into the background.

Artists in the past sometimes ignored size as a way to show spatial location. In looking at the manuscript illustration in **C**, we notice that the figures apparently at the "back" of the room are considerably larger in scale than those in the fore-

ground. This is not a mistake or lack of skill on the part of the artist. Often in the past, size was used to denote some conceptual importance and not to indicate how close or far away the figure was spatially. In **C** the figures of the kings and their ministers are portrayed larger simply to show their status as more important and powerful than that of the members of Parliament in the foreground, who are thus in smaller scale. This use of relative size to show importance and not space is called **hieratic scaling.** Although not naturalistic visually, this practice is quite common in art history. Images of gods, angels, saints, and rulers often arbitrarily were shown in a large size to indicate their thematic importance.

The use of size to denote depth is such a commonly recognized device that it is amusing to see a drawing such as **D**. Which figure is the largest? Of course, it's the one on the right! But measure it against the others; they're all the same size. This illusion occurs as all the other elements are diminishing in size in the "distance," and our brain is fooled. This shows how instinctively we use size difference to give an impression of space.

A Andō Hiroshige. *Boys' Day in Suidōbashi* from *One Hundred Famous Views of Edo.* 1857. Woodcut, 13¾ × 8⅞" (35 × 22.5). Courtesy Ronin Gallery, New York.

B Charles Henry Demuth. *Circus.* 1917. Watercolor and pencil on paper, 8¹/₁₆ × 13" (20.5 × 33 cm). Hirshhorn Museum and Sculpture Garden, Smithsonian Institution (gift of Joseph H. Hirshhorn Foundation, 1966).

C *Wriothesley.* Medieval manuscript. Windsor Castle, Royal Library. The Royal Collection © 1993 Her Majesty Queen Elizabeth II.

D Size-distance illusion.

A

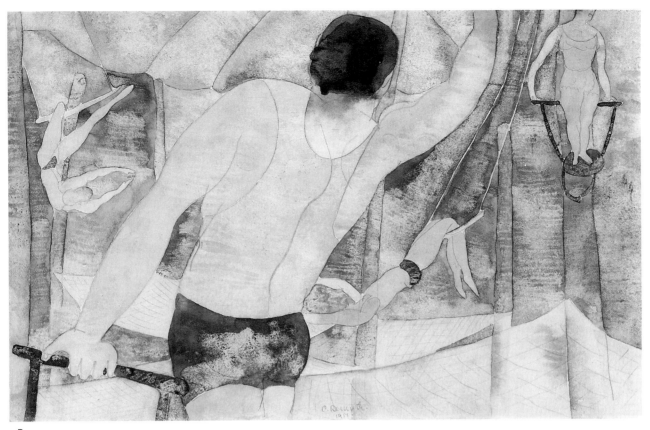

B

C

D

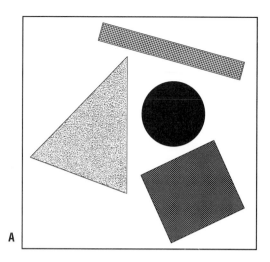

A

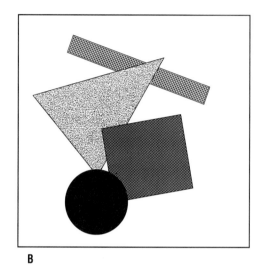

B

A No real feeling of space or depth can be discerned.
B Simple overlapping of the shapes establishes the spatial relationships.
C Jacob Lawrence. *Cabinet Makers.* 1946. Gouache with pencil underdrawing on paper, 21¾ × 30″ (55.2 × 76.1 cm). Hirshhorn Museum and Sculpture Garden, Smithsonian Institution (gift of Joseph H. Hirshhorn, 1966).
D Edith Hayller. *A Summer Shower.* 1883. Oil on board, 20 × 16¾″ (51 × 43 cm). Forbes Magazine Collection, New York.
E The design on bottom does not give as much feeling of spatial depth as the one on top.

C

DEVICES TO SHOW DEPTH

OVERLAPPING

Overlapping is a simple device for creating an illusion of depth. When we look at the design in **A**, we see four elements and have no way to judge their spatial relationships. In **B** the relationship is immediately clear due to overlapping. Each shape hides part of another because it is on top of or in front of the other. A sense of depth is established.

In Jacob Lawrence's painting (**C**), the five cabinet makers are shown with no size difference between the figures in the front and those in back. But we do understand their respective positions because of the overlapping that hides portions of the figures. Since overlapping is the primary spatial device used, the space created is admittedly very shallow. The pattern of two-dimensional shapes is stronger than an illusion of depth. Notice that when overlapping is combined with size differences, as in Hayller's painting (**D**), the spatial sensation is greatly increased.

The same principle can be illustrated with abstract shapes, as the designs in **E** show. The design on the top, which combines overlapping and size differences, gives a much more effective feeling of spatial recession.

SEE ALSO: *Transparency, page 195.*

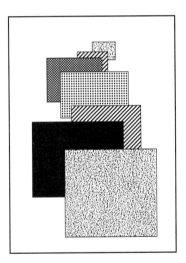

D

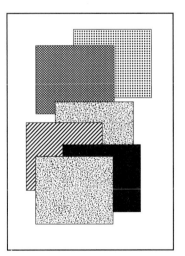

E

DEVICES TO SHOW DEPTH

VERTICAL LOCATION

Vertical location is a spatial device in which elevation on the page or format indicates a recession into depth. The *higher* an object, the farther back it is assumed to be. In the Persian miniature **(A)**, the various figures and objects are depicted with no differences in size, but with some overlapping. The artist is relying mainly on vertical location to give us a sense of recession into depth. To our eyes, the effect, though charming and decorative, seems to have little suggestion of depth. The figures appear to sit almost on top of each other all in one plane. However, this device was used widely in Near Eastern art and often in Oriental art and was immediately understandable in those cultures.

The spatially puzzling American painting in **B** shows the use of vertical location. Again this is about the only clue we have as to spatial position. There is some overlapping, but the differences in size are very arbitrary; buildings further away are shown larger than some apparently closer to us. It is only the vertical location placement that enables us even to think of foreground and background.

The painting by Sheeler **(C)** shows that this device can be effective even in quite naturalistic art. In this painting there is spatial overlapping but almost no size differences or value changes. Yet we automatically feel that the top of the picture is the ''background.'' We sense the space presented based mainly on vertical location.

Vertical location is based on a visual fact. As we stand and look at the scene before us, the closest place to us is the ground down at our feet. As we gradually raise our eyes upward, objects move further away until we reach what is called the **horizon,** or eye level. Thus, a horizon reference is an integral part of vertical location. In the twentieth century, we have gained the ability to fly, and the traditional ground–horizon–sky visual reference has been considerably altered. We are increasingly accustomed to aerial photographs or ''bird's-eye'' views **(D)** in which the traditional horizon has disappeared, and the point farthest from us can indeed be at the bottom of the picture. Vertical location is still an effective spatial device but not as automatically perceived as in the past.

A

B

C

A *Bahram Gur in the Turquoise Palace on Wednesday.*
   16th century. Persian miniature. Metropolitan
   Museum of Art, New York (gift of Alexander Smith
   Cochran, 1913; 13.228.7).
B Joseph Pickett. *Manchester Valley.* 1914–1918 (?).
   Oil with sand on canvas, 45½ × 60⅝″ (115.6 ×
   154 cm). The Museum of Modern Art, New York
   (gift of Abby Aldrich Rockefeller).
C Charles Sheeler. *Americana.* 1931. Oil on canvas,
   48 × 36″ (121.9 × 91.4 cm). The Metropolitan
   Museum of Art, New York (Edith and Milton
   Lowenthal Collection, bequest of Edith Abrahamson
   Lowenthal, 1992.24.8).
D Berenice Abbott. *Wall Street, Showing East River
   from Roof of Irving Trust Company.* 1938.
   Photograph. Museum of the City of New York.

D

DEVICES TO SHOW DEPTH

AERIAL PERSPECTIVE

Aerial, or **atmospheric, perspective** means the use of color and/or value (dark and light) to show depth. Example **A** illustrates the idea: The value contrast between distant objects gradually lessens, and contours become less distinct. The color would change also, with objects that are far away appearing more neutral in color and taking on a bluish character.

In **B** the feeling of spatial recession is based entirely on differences in size. Example **C** shows the same design, but the spatial feeling is greatly increased, since the smaller shapes become progressively darker and show less value contrast with the background.

We ordinarily think of aerial perspective and value changes to show distance as applied to vast landscapes with distant hills, as in **A**. But look at **D**. Of course, the overlapping immediately establishes that one woman is behind the other. But notice how the sense of depth is increased because of the sharp darks and lights on the closer figure. The back figure is done in grays, sometimes almost fading into the background color. Aerial perspective has many applications.
SEE ALSO: *Value and Space, page 218; Color and Space, page 242.*

A Ansel Adams. *Yosemite Valley from Inspiration Point.* Ca. 1936. Photograph. Copyright © 1993 by the Trustees of the Ansel Adams Publishing Rights Trust. All rights reserved.
B A feeling of spatial recession can be achieved simply by reducing the size of elements as they apparently recede into the distance.
C Spatial recession can be made even more effective if the receding objects blend more and more with the background.
D Louis Le Nain. *Two Seated Peasants.* Black crayon and sanguine with India ink washes on gray paper, 16⅛ × 11⅜″ (40.9 × 28.8 cm). Musée du Louvre, Paris.

A

B

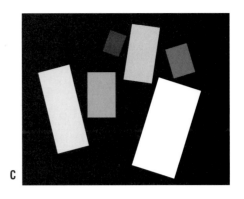

C

D

A

B

DEVICES TO SHOW DEPTH

LINEAR PERSPECTIVE

Linear perspective is a complex spatial system based on a relatively simple visual phenomenon: As parallel lines recede, they appear to converge and to meet on an imaginary line called the **horizon,** or **eye level.** We have all noticed this effect with railroad tracks or a highway stretching away into the distance. From this everyday visual effect, the whole "science" of linear perspective has developed. Artists had long noted this convergence of receding parallel lines, but not until the Renaissance was the idea introduced that parallel lines on parallel planes all converge at the same place (a **vanishing point**) on the horizon. The poster in **A** illustrates the idea. The parallel lines of the rails gradually taper, leading to one common point. The result is an effective impression of very deep space.

Linear perspective was a dominant device for spatial representation in Western art for several hundred years. It is easy to see why. First, linear perspective does approximate the visual image; it does appear "realistic" for artists striving to reproduce what the eye sees. Second, by its very nature, perspective acts as a unifying factor. With all the lines in **A** receding to a common point, a strong focus is created on the "north star" of the poster's title.

Because our view is of the corner of the gas station in **B**, the sloping parallel lines of the building would meet at *two* points on the low horizon line: the right one at the corner of the painting and the left one outside the format.

Although the introduction of, and continued fascination with, linear perspective as a spatial device was mainly a Western development, examples can be found from other cultures. The Japanese woodcut in **C** is an example. The diagonals of the room's floor, walls, and ceiling are clearly receding to a common vanishing point. This print combines a Western system of spatial depiction with the Japanese emphasis on two-dimensional shapes and patterns.

A A. M. Cassandre. *Étoile du Nord,* 1927. Poster, 47 × 30″ (120 × 75 cm). Reinhold-Brown Gallery, New York.

B Edward Ruscha. *Standard Station, Amarillo, Texas.* 1963. Oil on canvas, 5′5″ × 10′4″ (1.65 × 3.15 m). Hood Museum of Art, Dartmouth College, Hanover, N.H. (gift of James J. Meeker, Class of 1958, in memory of Lee English).

C Furuyama Moromasa. *Gama of Hand Sumō.* Ca. 1740. Woodblock print, 13 × 18½″ (33 × 47 cm). Metropolitan Museum of Art, New York (Frederick C. Hewitt Fund, 1911; JP 655).

C

A

B

A Dirk Bouts. *Last Supper Altarpiece,* detail. 1464–1467. Panel, 6′ × 5′ (l.83 × 1.53 m). Church of St. Pierre, Louvain.
B The basic structure of the painting in *A* involves all parallel lines converging at the same place.
C Ingo Swann. *Highways I.* 1976. Oil on canvas, 40 × 40″ (102 × 102 cm). National Air and Space Museum, Smithsonian Institution (gift of the artist).

DEVICES TO SHOW DEPTH

ONE-POINT PERSPECTIVE

The complete study of **linear perspective** is a complicated task. Entire books are devoted to it alone, and it cannot be fully described here. The procedures for using linear perspective were rediscovered and developed during the Renaissance period. From drawings, we see that in the fifteenth and sixteenth centuries many artists preceded paintings with careful perspective studies of the space involved.

Probably few recent painters have made such a strict use of linear perspective. For the architect, city planner, interior designer, set designer, and so on, an ability to do perspective drawing is essential for presenting their ideas. But it is important for any designer or artist to know the general principles of linear perspective for it is a valuable tool for representing an illusion of depth.

The concept of linear perspective starts with the placement of a horizontal line, the "horizon," that corresponds to the *eye level* of the artist. On this line are located the needed number of *vanishing points* to which lines or edges will be directed. It

might seem that working by a "formula" such as linear perspective provides would lead to a certain sameness and monotony in pictures. This is not true, because the artist's choice in the placement of the horizon and vanishing points on the format (or *outside* it) is almost unlimited. The same scene drawn by the same artist would result in radically different visual compositions by altering these initial choices.

Dirk Bouts' painting **(A)** is an example of what is called **one-point perspective.** A single point has been placed on the horizon line, and all the lines of objects at right angles to the plane of the canvas angle off toward that point. The lines of the walls, windows, ceiling beams, tiled floor, and even the table, if extended, would meet at this common point **(B)**. Then, in this created volume, the figures have been placed.

No diagram is needed to illustrate the one-point perspective used in **C**. A receding highway with the tapering sides meeting on the horizon is almost a visual cliché of using perspective. The artist Ingo Swann has taken this expected image and given it a different atmosphere befitting this age of space exploration and travel.

C

A

A   Antonio Canal Canaletto (1697–1798). *Santa Maria Zobenigo.* Oil on canvas, 18½ × 30⅝″ (47 × 78 cm). Private Collection.
B   The angled lines of the architecture would meet at two points on the horizon.
C   Edward Hopper. *El Palacio.* 1946. Watercolor on paper, 20¾ × 28⅝″ (53 × 73 cm). Collection of Whitney Museum of American Art, New York (exchange, 50.2).

B

DEVICES TO SHOW DEPTH

TWO-POINT PERSPECTIVE

One-point perspective presents a very organized and unified spatial image. **Two-point perspective** probably appears to us as more natural and lifelike. Here we are not looking ''head on'' at the scene. Now, it is being viewed from an angle. No objects are parallel to the picture plane and all edges recede to *two* points on the horizon line. This does more nearly approximate our usual visual experience.

The painting by Canaletto **(A)** illustrates the idea. In the diagram **(B)** the horizon line is shown on which there are two points and the various architectural lines of the different buildings recede to them.

In a perspective drawing or painting, the horizon line and the vanishing points obviously do not change. Thus, while extremely organized in a spatial sense, it can appear a bit posed and artificial. It assumes we are standing still and looking without moving. This is possible and does happen, but is not typical of our usual daily lives. Our visual knowledge is gained by looking at objects or scenes from many changing viewpoints. Perhaps for this reason, it is true that in painting, linear perspective is not used today as it was for centuries. For one thing, the camera now captures quickly and easily a static view. Many artists use the concepts of perspective as a guide, rendering a ''visual perspective'' without rigid adherence to the many rules **(C)**.

C

A

A George Tooker. *The Subway.* 1950. Egg tempera on composition board, 18 × 36″ (46 × 92 cm). Whitney Museum of American Art, New York (Juliana Force, purchase; 50.23).
B In *A* the angled corridors use several vanishing points.
C Giorgio de Chirico. *The Evil Genius of a King.* 1914–1915. Oil on canvas, 24 × 19¾″ (61 × 50.2 cm). The Museum of Modern Art, New York (purchase).

B

DEVICES TO SHOW DEPTH

MULTIPOINT PERSPECTIVE

In perspective drawing, the vertical edges of forms generally remain vertical. Sometimes a third vanishing point is added above (or below) the horizon so that the vertical parallels also taper and converge. This is useful to suggest great height, such as looking up at (or down from) a city skyscraper.

Although city streets or a line of buildings might be laid out in orderly rectangular rows of parallel lines, often in real life a variety of angles will be present. This entails the use of **multipoint perspective.** Different objects will have separate sets of vanishing points, though all will still be on a common horizon line. This can reproduce our visual experience where rarely in any scene are all the elements in neat, parallel placement. In the painting by Tooker **(A)** the long corridors of the subway recede back at several different angles from the center foreground. Each area thus has a separate vanishing point **(B)**.

The somewhat threatening feeling of the subway as a maze of confusing passageways is clearly presented.

When the vanishing points of multipoint perspective do not meet on a common horizon line, the impression is that the planes are slanted, inclined, or even floating. The painting by de Chirico **(C)** has a purposely confusing and ambiguous spatial effect. The edges of the foreground planes and background buildings draw closer as they recede, but the vanishing points would be widely divergent. The result is unsettling and strange.

Perspective is a traditional and visually understood method for presenting a three-dimensional impression on a flat surface. Except perhaps for some craft areas, there are few fields of art where at least a general understanding of perspective is not advantageous. In some design and illustration areas it is essential to have a technical knowledge of all the various types and procedures.

C

AMPLIFIED PERSPECTIVE

To introduce a dramatic, dynamic quality into their pictures, many artists have used what is called **amplified perspective.** This device reproduces the visual image, but in the very special view that occurs when an item is pointed directly at the viewer.

A familiar example is the old army recruiting poster, where Uncle Sam's pointing finger is thrust forward (''I Want You'') and right at the viewer. The same effect can be seen in **A**, in which the model thrusts her clenched hand directly at us. In this exaggerated example we are presented with the image of the hand being unbelievably large in juxtaposition with the body an arm's length away. The photograph heightens a phenomenon we see in less dramatic terms everyday but unconsciously adjust to conform with our knowledge of the human figure.

In Alexander Rodchenko's *At the Telephone* **(B)** we are presented with the top of the figure's head pointing directly at us. In this case we can see a **foreshortened** view of the receding body. The body looks shorter than we know it to be in profile, and we are shown a dramatic unfamiliar view of the figure.

The contrast of size we see in Andrew Wyeth's painting in **C** is similar in effect to that in **A**. The tree trunk points at us in large scale, receding almost immediately to the forest floor, where we see the tiny figure of the hunter. An advantage of amplified perspective is that the viewer's eye is pulled quickly into the picture. The composition in **C** exerts a dynamic pull inward from the close sycamore branches to the far figure. In this example a leaf can be the same size as a figure! With amplified perspective the spatial quality becomes the image's most eye-catching element. It is an effective tool for making the viewer forget that the picture is a flat, two-dimensional plane.

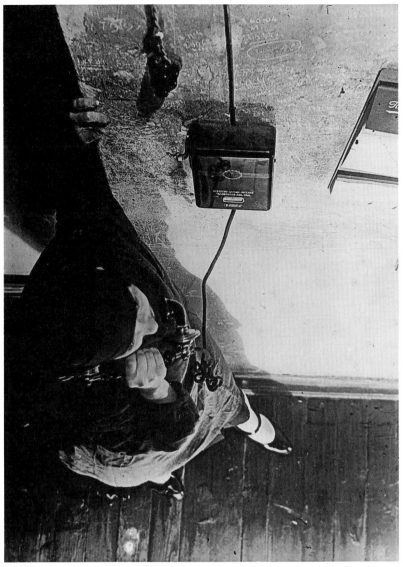

B

A Olga Vyleťalová. Poster for an exhibition of her work, 1980. Reproduced from: ''Czech Design,'' *Print* magazine, Jan/Feb 1991, p. 44. Courtesy of *Print.*

B Alexander Rodchenko. *At the Telephone.* 1928. Gelatin-silver print, 15½ × 11½" (39 × 29 cm). The Museum of Modern Art, New York (Mr. and Mrs. John Spencer Fund).

C Andrew Wyeth. *The Hunter.* 1943. Tempera on wood panel, 33 × 33⅞" (84 × 86 cm). Toledo Museum of Art (Elizabeth C. Mau Bequest Fund).

C

MULTIPLE PERSPECTIVE

Looking at a figure or object from more than one vantage point simultaneously is called **multiple perspective.** Several different views are combined in one image. This device has been used widely in twentieth-century art, although the idea is centuries old.

Multiple perspective was a basic pictorial device in Egyptian art, as illustrated in a typical Egyptian painted figure **(A)**. The artist's aim was not necessarily to reproduce the visual image, but to give a composite image combining the most descriptive or characteristic view of each part of the body. In **B**, which view of the head is most descriptive, which most certainly a head? The profile obviously says "head" more clearly. But what about the eye **(C)**? The eye in profile is a confusing shape, but the front view is what we know as an eye. The Egyptians solved this problem by combining a side view of the head with a front view of the eye. Each body part is thus presented in its most characteristic aspect: a front view of the torso, a side view of the legs, and so forth.

Much the same reasoning probably inspired the nineteenth-century American artist in the charming drawing of a Pennsylvania farm **(D)**. Fields, barn, house, orchard, and so on, are seen from different viewpoints, but each presents the clearest, most typical aspect.

In the twentieth century, with the camera able to give us effortlessly the fixed visual ("realistic") view, artists have been freed to explore other avenues of perception including multiple perspective. In fact the artist David Hockney has even liberated the camera from its usual limitation as a "frozen Cyclops." Hockney's photo-collage of *The Brooklyn Bridge* **(E)** presents multiple perspectives, from a view including his feet, to one looking upwards. The composite of views makes curves of straight lines and fractures the image much like a cubist painting.

As you have noticed, multiple perspective does not give a clear spatial pattern of the position occupied by each element. This aspect has been sacrificed to give a more subjective, conceptual view of forms.

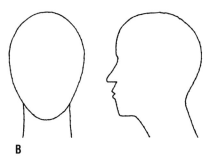

B

A

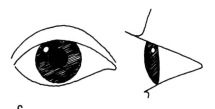

C

D

E

A *The Sculptor Ipuy and His Wife,* detail of Egyptian wall painting (restored). Ca. 1275 B.C. Tomb of Ipuy, Deir el Medina. Metropolitan Museum of Art, New York, 30.4.114.

B To the Egyptians, the head shown in profile seemed to be the most characteristic view.

C The front view of the eye gives the clearest, most descriptive view.

D Anonymous (American). *Pennsylvania Farmstead with Many Fences.* Early 19th century. Pen and watercolor, 18 × 23⅞″ (45 × 59.6 cm). Courtesy Museum of Fine Arts, Boston (M. and M. Karolik Collection).

E David Hockney. *The Brooklyn Bridge, November 28th 1982.* Photographic collage, 109 × 58″ (277 × 147 cm). © David Hockney.

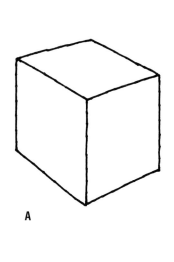

A

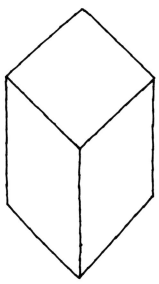

B

C

D

ISOMETRIC PROJECTION

For centuries Oriental artists did not make wide use of linear perspective. Another spatial convention was satisfactory for their pictorial purposes. In Oriental art, planes recede on the diagonal, but the lines, instead of drawing closer together, remain parallel. Example **A** shows a box drawn in linear perspective; **B** shows the box drawn in the Oriental method. In the West we refer to image **B** as an **isometric projection.**

A typical Japanese print (**C**) illustrates this device. The effect is different, but certainly not disturbing. The rather flat decorative effect seems perfectly in keeping with the treatment of the figures, with their strong linear pattern and flat color areas. The artist does not stress three-dimensional solidity or roundness in the figures, so we do not miss this quality in the background. Oriental art rarely stressed the strictly visual impression of the world. The art was more subjective, more evoc-

ative than descriptive of the natural world. Linear perspective was undoubtedly not needed for the expressive aims of these artists.

Isometric projection, while used extensively in engineering and mechanical drawings, is rarely seen in Western painting. The self-portrait by David Hockney (**D**) uses this device, and the change from the linear perspective is fresh and intriguing.

The work by Josef Albers (**E**) uses this idea in a purely abstract way. The artist creates a geometric shape drawn in an isometric-type view. The interesting aspect of the design, however, is the shifting, puzzling spatial pattern that emerges. The direction of any plane seems to advance, then recede, then to be flat in a fascinating ambiguity.

A In linear perspective, parallel lines gradually draw closer together as they recede into the distance.

B In isometric projection, parallel lines remain parallel.

C Katsushika Hokusai. *Poem by Ise, A Lady of the 9th Century* (from The Hundred Poems Explained by the Nurse, No. 19). Ca. 1839. Woodblock print, 10½ × 14¾″ (27 × 37 cm). The Metropolitan Museum of Art, New York (Rogers Fund, 1936; JP 2548).

D David Hockney. *Self Portrait with Blue Guitar.* 1977. Oil on canvas, 5′ × 6′ (1.52 × 1.83 cm). © David Hockney.

E Josef Albers. *Structural Constellation II.* Ca. 1950. Machine-engraved vinylite mounted on board, 17 × 22½″ (43.2 × 57.1 cm). Collection, The Josef Albers Foundation.

E

OPEN FORM/CLOSED FORM

One other aspect of pictorial space is of concern to the artist or designer. This is the concept of *enclosure,* the use of what is referred to as **open form** or **closed form.** The artist has the choice of giving us a complete scene or merely a partial glimpse of a portion of a scene that continues beyond the format. In **A** Chardin puts the focal point in the center of the composition, and our eyes are not led out of the painting. The still life of musical instruments and sheet music is effectively framed by the curved border of the picture, which echoes the many ovals in the composition. The book on the left and the candle on the right "bracket" the composition and keep our attention within the picture. This is called closed form.

By contrast, example **B** is clearly open form. In these postage stamps only partial glimpses of the figure are seen, and all these lead the eye off the format. In fact, this design almost forces us to think more of the parts we *cannot* see than of those shown in the picture. This design solution is appropriate to the subject of athletic action.

The ultimate extension of the open-form concept is illustrated in **C**. This painting has actual elements that extend outside the rectangular format and effectively destroy any framed, or contained feeling. In fact, it is almost as if the painting has spawned smaller paintings which leap out from the "frame."

Throughout history it has been customary to frame paintings. A **frame** is a border around the perimeter that visually turns the eye inward. Thus, frames created the effect of closed form, no matter what the original design of the artwork. Some artists have gone even further and included painted "frames" (and even lettered titles) as elements within the composition **(D)**.

As you can see, closed form generally gives a rather formal, structured appearance, whereas open form creates a casual, momentary feeling, with elements moving on and off the format in an informal manner.

A

B

A Jean-Baptiste-Siméon Chardin. *The Attributes of Music.* 1765. Oil on canvas, 35⅞ × 56⅞″ (91 × 145 cm). Musée du Louvre, Paris.
B Stamp design © 1992, U.S. Postal Service. All Rights Reserved. Courtesy United States Olympic Committee.
C Elizabeth Murray. *Truth, Justice and Comics #2.* 1990. Oil on canvas, 48⅜ × 41¾ × 3¾″ (123 × 106 × 10 cm). Courtesy Paula Cooper Gallery, New York.
D Neil Jenney. *North America Abstracted.* 1980. Oil on wood, 3′ × 7′1¼″ (0.92 × 2.17 m). Whitney Museum of American Art, New York (purchase; 83.19).

C

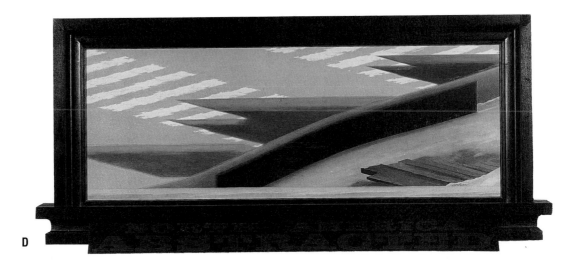

D

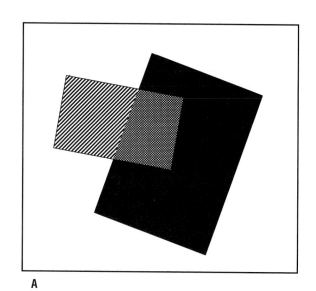

A

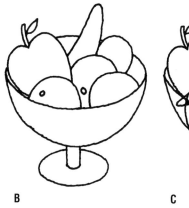

B

C

D

TRANSPARENCY

EQUIVOCAL SPACE

Most art in the twentieth century has not been concerned with a purely naturalistic reproduction of the world around us. Photography has provided a way we can all record appearance in a picture. This is true in the area of spatial and depth representation also. Many artists have chosen to ignore the device of overlapping. Instead, they have used what is called **transparency.** When two forms overlap and both are seen completely, the figures are assumed to be "transparent" **(A)**.

Transparency does *not* give us a clear spatial pattern. In **A** we are not sure which form is on top and which behind. The spatial pattern can change as we look at it. This purposeful ambiguity is called **equivocal space,** and many artists find it a more interesting visual pattern than the immediately clear spatial organization provided by overlapping in a design.

There is another rationale for the use of transparency. Just because one item is in front and hides another object does not mean the item in back has ceased to exist. In **B** a bowl of fruit is depicted with the customary visual device of overlapping. In **C** the same bowl of fruit is shown with transparency, and we discover another piece of fruit in the bottom of the bowl. It was always there, simply hidden from our view. So, which design is more "realistic"? By what standards do you decide?

The sweatshirt design in **D** was done on a computer. Created to celebrate a fifth anniversary, the letters of "FIVE" are clear. But they overlap and become transparent with differing visual textures. The design takes a simple theme and creates an interesting pattern from a few elements.

The screenprint by Andy Warhol **(E)** is an arrangement of one image (the familiar *Mona Lisa*) repeated in various sizes. Spatial interest is increased by using transparency in many places so the forms interpenetrate rather than get hidden by the more usual overlapping technique.

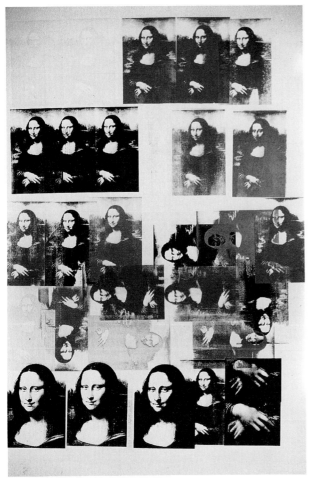

E

A The use of overlapping with transparency confuses our perception of depth.

B Overlapping sometimes can be deceptive.

C The use of transparency reveals what is hidden by overlapping.

D Sweatshirt Design for a Fifth Anniversary. 1990. Designer: Jennifer Bartlett; Design firm: Vickerman-Zachary-Miller, Oakland, CA.

E Andy Warhol. *Colored Mona Lisa.* 1963. Silkscreen ink on synthetic polymer paint on canvas, 10'8" × 6'10" (3.25 × 2.08 m). © 1993 The Andy Warhol Foundation for the Visual Arts, Inc.

A

B

A Giovanni Battista Piranesi. *The Prisons.* Ca. 1750. Intaglio, 21⅜ × 16¼″ (54 × 41 cm). The Metropolitan Museum of Art, New York (Harris Brisbane Dick Fund, 1937; 37.45.3.27).

B René Magritte. *The Blank Signature.* 1965. Oil on canvas, 32 × 25⅝″ (81.3 × 65.1 cm). © 1993 National Gallery of Art (collection of Mr. and Mrs. Paul Mellon).

C M. C. Escher. *Relativity.* 1953. Lithograph. (1993) National Gallery of Art, Washington, DC (Cornelius Van S. Roosevelt Collection).

SPATIAL PUZZLES

Artists all have learned the various devices to give an illusion of depth or space. At times certain artists purposely ignore these conventions to provide an unexpected image. A confusion of spatial relationships is intriguing because the viewer is confronted with a visual puzzle rather than a statement.

Piranesi, in one of his many etchings of prisons (**A**), not only ignores the ''rules'' but actually distorts them to create a weird, spatially intricate scene. The confused, mazelike complexity of the enormous chamber serves as an ominous symbol of government bureaucracy and repression.

Example **B** is a Surrealist painting. The whole thrust of surrealism was to illustrate the impossible world of dreams and the subconscious mind. The Magritte painting in **B** has a very simple, straightforward subject. But the picture is intriguing because the spatial relationships are all confused. Subject and background are not separate. They become one as they replace each other at unexpected places.

The lithograph in **C** has a similar feeling to **A**. The artist, M. C. Escher, has produced many works that purposely employ this confusion of spatial relationships. His work is fascinating as, at first glance, the careful rendering and brilliant draftsmanship seem to present a straightforward scene. The picture in **C** is filled with stairways and figures that go up and down. But there is no logical relationship and no way we can discern any regular spatial pattern.

C

11

ILLUSION OF MOTION

A

B

INTRODUCTION

Change and movement are basic characteristics of existence. Our world is a world of movement. Almost every aspect of life involves constant change. We humans cannot sit or stand motionless for more than a moment or so; even in sleep we turn and change position. But if we could stop our body movements, the world about us would still continue to change. Thus motion is an important consideration in art.

In this century, with the advent of rapid forms of transportation and communication, a significant number of artworks have reflected an interest in speed or motion. The Italian Futurists, in the second decade of this century, said the speeding automobile had replaced Venus de Milo as a standard of beauty. Some artworks, such as mobiles or mechanized sculptures, actually move; we apply the term **kinetic** to them.

Recent art and technology have also revealed new images from a world in motion. Photography has made visible images that are otherwise invisible to us due to a motion too rapid for the eye to perceive. Harold Edgerton's photograph of a milk droplet **(A)** reveals an instant of perfection when a crown is formed. Edgerton pioneered techniques of strobe lighting, which coordinates the camera with an instant of light to capture such images.

Only the movies or television can actually show us "moving pictures." In paintings or drawings that are static images, any feeling of motion or change is always merely a suggestion or an illusion. This illusion, however, has intrigued artists of many periods and countries.

The paintings shown in **B** and **C** have a great many visual differences. But they both are twentieth-century attempts to present a feeling of motion. In the painting by de Kooning **(B)** our eyes dart rapidly around the canvas following the complicated pattern of the vigorous, spontaneous brushstrokes. This is an example of Abstract Expressionism (also called "Action Painting"—an apt description, for we can sense the physical activity of the artist in creating the painting). This style has movement and dynamic excitement as primary goals.

Bridget Riley's painting **(C)**, shows a very different technique. It is a controlled, simply repetitive pattern of definite, hard-edged curving lines. But when we stare at it, the edges begin to blur and the lines begin to "swim," as the black and white areas vibrate. Even the painting's surface appears no longer flat, but seems to undulate and become a rippling surface. This type of painting is called Op Art, images that give optical illusions of movement in static images.

Two paintings quite dissimilar have the same goal—an illusion of motion.

C

A Harold E. Edgerton. *Milk-Drop Coronet.* 1957. Photograph. Estate of Harold E. Edgerton, courtesy of Palm Press, Inc.

B Willem de Kooning. *Composition.* 1955. Oil, enamel and charcoal on canvas, 6'7⅛" × 5'9⅛" (2.01 × 1.76 m). Solomon R. Guggenheim Museum, New York.

C Bridget Riley. *Current.* 1964. Synthetic polymer paint on composition board, 4'10⅜" × 4'10⅞" (1.48 × 1.5 m). The Museum of Modern Art, New York (Philip Johnson Fund).

ANTICIPATED MOVEMENT

Much of the implication of movement present in art is caused by our memory and past experience. We recognize temporary, unstable body positions and realize that change must be imminent. For example, we immediately "see" the action shown in **A**. The plantation workers are in poses that we recognize as momentary, and we anticipate the change that is imminent. By contrast the land owner is depicted at rest as he watches the laborers.

In a process called **kinesthetic empathy,** we tend to re-create unconsciously in our own bodies the actions we observe. We actually "feel" in our muscles the exertions of the athlete or dancer; we simultaneously stretch, push, or lean, though we are only watching. This involuntary reaction also applies to static images in art, where it can enhance the feeling of movement.

A feeling of movement can be heightened by contrast. Again, by memory, we realize that some things move and some do not. Thus in **B** the figures seem to have more activity, more

potential for movement, in their mobile positions because of the contrast with the large, solid building that appears so immobile. Our experience tells us that people move but buildings rarely do.

Even nonobjective patterns can display movement through contrast. Because of past experience, we also see horizontal lines as quiet and inactive—just as our bodies are resting and still when we are lying horizontally. For a similar reason we identify diagonal lines as suggestive of movement—just as our bodies lean and bend in such vigorous activities as sports. The horizontal emphasis of the buildings in **B** imparts a static feeling. But pure lines without subject reference can give the same result. A painting such as **C** seems dynamic and motion-filled. Here there are no recognizable objects, no forms that we can identify as being in fleeting positions. Yet we immediately sense not only the diagonal emphasis but also the rapid, spontaneous strokes of the artist's brush in creating the painting.

A Diego Rivera. *Sugar Cane*. 1931. Frescoed panel, 58″ (147 cm) high. Philadelphia Museum of Art (gift of Mr. and Mrs. Herbert Cameron Morris).
B Nicholas Poussin. *The Rape of the Sabine Women*. Ca. 1636–1637. Oil on canvas, 5′1″ × 6′10½″ (1.55 × 2.1 m). Metropolitan Museum of Art, New York (Harris Brisbane Dick Fund, 1946; 46.160).
C Michael Larionov. *Rayonist Composition: Domination of Red*. 1912–1913. Oil on canvas, 20¾ × 28½″ (53 × 72 cm). The Museum of Modern Art, New York (gift of the artist).

A

B

C

WAYS TO SUGGEST MOTION

FIGURE REPEATED

Over the centuries artists have devised various conventions to present an illusion of motion in art. One of the oldest devices is that of **repeating a figure.** As the thirteenth-century illumination in **A** illustrates, the figure of David from the Bible appears in different positions and situations. Architectural elements divide the format into four areas. In the upper left area David with his slingshot meets the giant Goliath and prepares for battle. To the upper right David cuts off the slain giant's head as the Philistine soldiers leave. David presents the head to the King of Israel in the lower left vignette, and in the final scene David receives the gift of a cloak from an admirer.

  This repetitive device was used widely in Oriental cultures as well as in Western medieval art. The figure of Krishna appears over and over in different positions and situations in the Indian miniature **(B)**. It is interesting to note that this very old technique is still popular. The comic strips in our newspapers use exactly the same idea. In a series of boxes we follow our favorite cartoon characters through a sequence of situations that relate a story.

  Often the repeated figure, rather than being shown in a sequence of small pictures, merely reappears in one unified composition. This device occurred in Oriental art, was adopted in Western art, and remained popular as late as the Renaissance. Usually a distinctive costume or color identified the repeated character, so that the repetition would be visually obvious. We see this in **C**, which recounts the familiar Biblical story of Salome. Three separate episodes are combined in one panel. In the right foreground Salome dances before Herod. At the far left John the Baptist is beheaded, and then to the right Salome presents his head on a platter. Because all the action is combined in one composition, we might miss the sequential aspect without more than casual observation.

  Sometimes we think of this technique of repeating a figure as confined only to medieval art, such as **C**. But the illustration in **D** shows it can still be an effective and eye-catching device today.

A *David Slays Goliath and Cuts Off His Head.* Manuscript illumination (M638 f 28v) from *Old Testament Miniatures*, Paris. Ca. 1245–1250. Tempera on vellum. The Pierpont Morgan Library, New York.

B *Krishna Revealing His Nature as Vishnu.* Miniature from Malwa, India. Ca. 1730. Gouache or watercolor on paper, 8 × 14¾″ (20 × 38 cm). Victoria and Albert Museum, London. Crown Copyright.

C Anonymous (Italian). *The Feast of Herod.* Ca. 1365. Tempera on wood, tooled gold ground, 17¹¹⁄₁₆ × 19½″ (45 × 49.5 cm). The Metropolitan Museum of Art, New York (Robert Lehman Collection, 1975.1.103).

D *Murder at the Pentagon.* 1993. Tobi Indyke, Art Director; Doubleday Book & Music Club, client; Joe Baker, photo-illustration.

A

B

C

D

WAYS TO SUGGEST MOTION

BLURRED OUTLINES

We readily interpret a photograph such as the one in **A** as a symbol of movement. With a fast shutter speed, moving images are frozen in "stop-action" photographs. Here the shutter speed is relatively slow, so that the skater becomes a blurred image that we read as an indication of the subject's movement. This is an everyday visual experience. When objects move through our field of vision quickly, we do not get a clear mental picture of them. A car will pass us on the highway so fast that we perceive only a colored blur. Details and edges of the form are lost in the rapidity of the movement.

The figure in the 16th-century Italian drawing (**B**) suggests movement in this way. The dancer is drawn with sketchy, incomplete, and overlapping lines to define her form.

The painting in **C** gives us a blurred view of an expanse of sky as a rainstorm begins. The falling water of the deluge is suggested with shapes and lines that have blurred edges.

Even in purely nonobjective paintings, the blurred edge serves as an effective device. The vertical sweeping shapes in **D** clearly suggest flowing and rapid movement. In **C** the deluge is a depicted one. In **D** we have a visual record of an actual "deluge" of paint controlled by the artist.

A

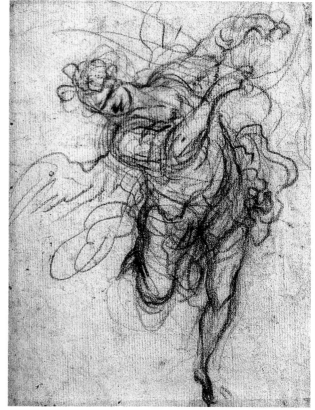

B

C

A Cynthia Torp. *Skater*. 1993. Lindgren & Smith Inc., New York.

B Anonymous (Italian). *Dancing Figure*. 16th century. Red chalk, 6¼ × 5¼″ (16 × 13 cm). Metropolitan Museum of Art, New York (gift of Cornelius Vanderbilt, 1880; 80.3.72).

C John Constable. *Seascape Study with Rain Clouds*. 1824. Oil on paper laid on canvas, 8¾ × 12¼″ (22.2 × 31 cm). Royal Academy of Arts, London.

D Morris Louis. *Saraband*. 1959. Acrylic on canvas, 8′6″ × 12′5″ (2.57 × 3.78 m). Solomon R. Guggenheim Museum, New York.

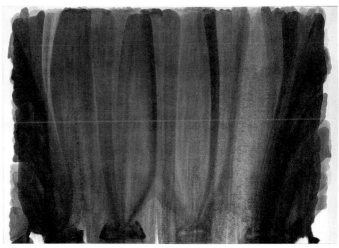

D

A

B

C

WAYS TO SUGGEST MOTION

MULTIPLE IMAGE

Another device for suggesting movement is called **multiple image,** illustrated in **A.** When we see one figure in an overlapping sequence of poses, the slight change in each successive position suggests movement taking place. Example **A** is a photograph from the 1880s. The photographer, Thomas Eakins, was intrigued with the camera's capabilities for answering the visual problem of showing movement and analyzing it.

Example **B** shows this idea in a drawing by Ingres. While Ingres' motive was probably just to try two different positions for the figure, we get a clear suggestion of the figure moving in dance-like gestures.

Painters of the twentieth century have often been concerned with finding a visual language to express the increasingly dynamic quality of the world around us. Although at first glance very different, Duchamp's famous *Nude Descending a Staircase* **(C)** is much like the Eakins photograph in **A.** Again, multiple images of a figure are shown to suggest a body's movement in progress. Now the body forms are abstracted into simple geometric forms that repeat diagonally down the canvas as the nude "descends." Many curved lines (called **lines of force**) are added to show the pathway of movement. This is a device we commonly see, and immediately understand, in today's comic strips.

The poster shown in **D** demonstrates a subtle use of multiple image to suggest a turning of the head. All that is required to convey this movement is a profile silhouette behind the three-quarter view portrait.

D

A Thomas Eakins. *Man Pole-Vaulting.* Ca. 1884. Photograph. Metropolitan Museum of Art, New York (gift of Charles Bregler, 1941; 41.142.11).

B Jean Auguste Dominique Ingres. *Female Nude.* Ca. 1826–1834. Pencil on white paper, 10⅞ × 11½″ (27.8 × 29.6 cm). Musée Bonnat, Bayonne.

C Marcel Duchamp. *Nude Descending a Staircase, No. 2.* 1912. Oil on canvas, 4′10″ × 2′11″ (1.47 × 0.89 m). Philadelphia Museum of Art (Louise and Walter Arensberg Collection).

D Poster for American Masters I: Gene Federico. Copyright © 1992 American Institute of Graphic Arts/New York Chapter. Design: Michael Gericke, Pentagram Design.

12

VALUE

INTRODUCTION

Value is simply the artistic term for light and dark. An area's value is its relative lightness or darkness in a given context. Only through changes of light and dark can we perceive anything. Light reveals forms; in a dark room at night we see nothing and bump into furniture and walls. The page you are reading now is legible only because the darkness of the type contrasts with the whiteness of the background paper. Even the person (or animal) who is physiologically unable to perceive color can function with only minimal difficulties by perception based on varying tones of gray.

Example **A** is a scale of seven values of gray. These are termed **achromatic** grays, as they are mixtures of only black and white; no color (or chroma) is used.

The term **value-contrast** refers to the relationship between areas of dark and light. Because the scale in **A** is arranged in sequential order, the contrast between any two adjoining areas is rather slight and termed *low-value* contrast. The center gray circles are all the same middle value. It is interesting to note how this consistent center gray seems to change visually depending on the background. Indeed, it is hard to believe that the circles on the far left and far right are precisely the same value.

The scale in **A** shows only seven basic steps. Theoretically, between black and white there could be an almost unlimited number of steps. Studies have shown that the average eye can discern somewhere around forty variations in value. The artist may use as many or as few values as his artistic purposes indicate, though at times the nature of the chosen medium may influence the result. The drawing of the interior in **B** uses a very broad range of values. The artist, Charles Sheeler, drawing with a conté crayon, skillfully exploited the medium's softness to create many grays and an interesting design of dark and light contrasts.

Value and color are related. Color, based on wavelengths of light, offers a much broader field of visual differences and contrasts. But grayed neutrals (now called **chromatic** grays) can also be produced by mixing certain colors, which result in different tones than those in **A**. A further relationship of value and color is that every color is, in itself, also simultaneously a certain value. Pure yellow is a light (high-value) color corresponding to a very light gray in terms of light reflection. Purple is basically a dark, low-value color that would match a very dark gray.

The early American painting in **C** does not begin to have the range of values seen in **B**. Here, in fact, there are perhaps only two or three value changes with almost no subtle gradations from dark to light. Yet the theme is perfectly understandable. A color reproduction would add some interest, but showing only the values makes a readable image. This reproduction shows what is called the *value pattern* of the original painting.

A   A value scale of gray. The center circles are identical in value.

B   Charles Sheeler. *The Open Door.* 1932. Conté crayon on paper, mounted on cardboard, 23¾ × 18″ (60.7 × 46.7 cm). The Metropolitan Museum of Art, New York (Edith and Milton Lowenthal Collection, bequest of Edith Abrahamson Lowenthal, 1992.24.7).

C   Anonymous (American). *The Quilting Party.* Late 19th century. Oil on wood, 13 × 25″ (33.4 × 63.6 cm). Abby Aldrich Rockefeller Folk Art Center.

A

B

C

A

B

VALUE PATTERN

In describing paintings or designs, we speak often of their **value pattern.** This term refers to the arrangement and the amount of variation in light and dark, independent of the colors used.

When value contrast is minimized and all the values are within a limited range with only small variation, the result is a restrained, subtle effect. The impression is one of understatement, whether the value range is limited to lights (*high* key is a term used often) or darks (*low* key). In Richard Dadd's watercolor **(A)**, the values are all extremely light, with really no contrasting dark areas, just a few slightly darker lines here and there. The painting in **B** shows the opposite approach, an extreme contrast of dark and light. This is a Baroque painting, done in a period when artists purposely accentuated value contrasts to portray exciting themes. The violent and gory subject of Artemisia Gentileschi's painting **(B)** receives an aptly emotional visual treatment. The candlelit picture has dramatic, sudden shadows throughout the scene, achieving an almost theatrical effect.

Our different responses to **A** and **B** illustrate how value alone can create an immediate emotional reaction. The artist can choose a value pattern to elicit emotional reactions in the viewer. Closely related values are calm and quiet. The theme of the harem in **A** is shown with unnaturally light values, and the shapes are barely discernible. An exotic, mystical, almost magical mood results. On the other hand, sharp value contrasts suggest drama, excitement, even conflict. Certainly, the gruesome theme of **B** would not be communicated by the limited range of values in **A**. An entirely different mood would have been presented.

In the same way overall darkness may provide feelings of sadness, depression, and even mystery. Lighter values, being brighter, seem less serious or threatening. Specific colors will always evoke emotional reactions, but the value pattern alone can be important in expressing a theme.

The painting in **B** shows values that could be seen in a dark room lit only by candles. The painting in **C** does not refer to any specific light source but involves also an extreme contrast of light and dark. The artist here has deliberately exaggerated (or "heightened") the value contrast. The shapes have been simplified into a pattern of mostly black and white with only a few gray areas. This produces an unusual and highly dramatic image of what could have seemed a rather ordinary scene if done with a naturalistic value pattern.

A   Richard Dadd. *Fantasie de l'Harem Égyptien.* 1865. Watercolor, 10⅞ × 7″ (48 × 18 cm). Ashmolean Museum, Oxford.

B   Artemisia Gentileschi. *Judith Decapitating Holofernes.* Ca. 1620. Oil on canvas, 79 × 60″ (199 × 152.5 cm). Galleria degli Uffizi, Florence.

C   Robert Harvey. *Brother Home on Leave.* 1964. Oil on canvas, 48″ (121.9 cm) square. Courtesy of the Mead Corporation, Dayton, OH.

C

VALUE AS EMPHASIS

A valuable use of dark-and-light contrast is to create a focal point or center of attention in a design. A visual emphasis or "starting point" is often desired. A thematically important character or feature can be visually emphasized by value contrast. High dark-and-light contrast instantly attracts our attention. By planning high contrast in one area and subdued contrast elsewhere, the artist can be assured where the viewer's eye will be directed first.

Whistler's painting *At the Piano* **(A)** directs the eye immediately to the young girl on the right. Her light dress stands in bold contrast to the darkness of the space around her, including the piano. On the other hand the woman playing the piano is "absorbed" into the dark background.

Rosa Bonheur's *The Horse Fair* **(B)** places emphasis on the light horses against the darker background. However, our attention does not remain fixed on this focal point. The receding row of trees leads us back to the left side of the painting where the activity redirects our attention back toward the eye-catching white horses. In this picture a strong emphasis is balanced by a composition that keeps the eye moving.

Edward Hopper's *Nighthawks* **(C)** emphasizes the interior of a brightly lit cafe. The sharp white interior contrasts with the darkness outside. This light then "frames" the several dark figures, who become the focal point of the painting. The general isolation of these dark spots reinforces the quiet, almost melancholy mood of the painting.

All of these paintings are, of course, done in color. But the black-and-white reproductions here are valuable to show the artists' reliance on value contrast, irrespective of the particular colors involved. Most artists are as aware of the value pattern they create as the pattern of various colors. The artistic choice is often not green or red but how dark (or light) a green or red to use.

A

B

A James McNeill Whistler. *At the Piano.* 1858–59. Oil on canvas, 26⅜ × 36¹⁄₁₆″ (67 × 92 cm). Taft Museum, Cincinnati (bequest of Louise Taft Semple, 1962.7).

B Rosa Bonheur. *The Horse Fair.* 1853. Oil on canvas, 96¼ × 199½″ (244.5 × 406.8 cm). The Metropolitan Museum of Art, New York (gift of Cornelius Vanderbilt, 1887.25).

C Edward Hopper. *Nighthawks.* 1942. Oil on canvas, 2′6″ × 5′ (0.76 × 1.44 m). Photograph courtesy of The Art Institute of Chicago (Friends of American Art Collection, 1942.51).

C

VALUE AND SPACE

One of the most important uses of gradations of dark and light is to suggest volume or space.

On a flat surface value can be used to impart a three-dimensional quality to shapes. During the Renaissance the word **chiaroscuro** was coined to describe the artistic device of using light and dark to imply depth and volume in a painting or drawing. *Chiaroscuro* is a combination of the Italian words for "light" and "dark." A drawing using only line is very effective in showing shapes. By varying the weight of the line, an artist may imply dimension or solidity, but the effect is subtle. When areas of dark and light are added, we begin to feel the three-dimensional quality of forms. This is apparent in Michelangelo's *Madonna and Child* **(A)**. The baby has been shaded in dark and light, giving it a feeling of volume and three dimensions, especially in comparison with the figure of the Madonna. Being drawn just in line, she remains a fairly flat portrayal.

Artists constantly use value differences (or shading) to suggest three-dimensional form on a flat surface. The watercolor in **B** shows how effectively the feeling of volume and space can be presented.

In **C** the artist, Albright, has greatly exaggerated slight visual changes in value. The result is a lumpy, almost decayed,

feeling to the flesh. This painting shows that value can be used to provoke an emotional response.

Much art has been, and is, concerned with producing a simulation of our three-dimensional world. On a two-dimensional piece of paper or canvas, an *illusion* of space is desired—and perhaps not just the roundness of a head but a whole scene receding far into the distance. Here again the use of value can be a valuable tool of the artist. High-value contrast seems to come forward, to be actually *closer,* whereas areas of lesser contrast recede or stay back, suggesting distance. Notice how effectively Caspar Friedrich has used this technique in painting **D**. The figure on the rocks in front is sharply dark against the rest of the picture. Then each receding rock, wave, and bit of land becomes progressively lighter and closer to the value of the sky. An illusion of great depth is thus created by manipulating the various values. This technique does reproduce what our eyes see: Far-off images visually become grayer and less distinct as the distance increases. In art, this is called **aerial perspective** or **atmospheric perspective.**

A Michelangelo. *Madonna and Child.* 1535–40 (?). Black and red chalk and white pigment on prepared paper, 21⅜ × 15⅝″ (54 × 40 cm). Casa Buonarotti, Florence.

B Sue Hettmansperger. *Untitled.* 1975. Watercolor and pencil, 23 × 25″ (58 × 64 cm). North Carolina National Bank.

C Ivan Le Lorraine Albright. *Three Love Birds.* 1930. Charcoal on canvas, 78½ × 42″ (199.4 × 106.7 cm). Photograph courtesy of The Art Institute of Chicago (gift of Ivan Albright, 1977.38).

D Caspar David Friedrich. *The Wanderer Above the Sea of Mist.* Ca. 1817–1818. Oil on canvas, 38⅜ × 29¼″ (99 × 75 cm). Kunsthalle, Hamburg.

A

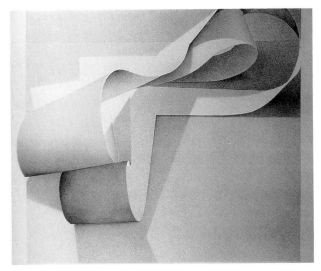

B

C

D

A Pierre Paul Prud'hon. *La Source.* Ca. 1801. Black and white chalk on blue-gray paper, 21³⁄₁₆ × 15⁵⁄₁₆″ (54 × 39 cm). Sterling and Francine Clark Art Institute, Williamstown, MA.

B Henri Matisse. *Standing Woman Seen from Behind.* 1909. Pen and ink, 10½ × 8⅝″ (27 × 22 cm). The Museum of Modern Art, New York (Carol Buttenweiser Loeb Memorial Fund).

C Vincent van Gogh. *Washerwomen on the Canal.* 1888. Pen and ink, 12½ × 9½″ (31.5 × 24 cm). Rijksmuseum Kröller-Müller, Otterlo.

D Georges Seurat. *Seated Boy With Straw Hat.* (Study for *The Bathers*). 1882. Conté crayon, 9½ × 12¼″ (24.13 × 31.1 cm). Yale University Art Gallery, New Haven (Everett V. Meeks Fund).

E *Untitled.* 1991. Illustrator: Max Seabaugh; Design firm: Adobe Systems, Inc.

A

B

C

TECHNIQUES

The use of value in a work of art is what we would commonly call **shading.** However, to say that an artist uses shading does little to describe the final work, as there are so many techniques and hence many visual effects available. Artistic aims vary from producing a naturalistic rendition of some visual image to a completely nonobjective work that uses dark and light simply as an element to provide added visual interest to the design. Even with a similar purpose, the same subject done by the same artist will be very different depending on the chosen medium and technique. These examples can show you just a few of the almost unlimited possibilities.

Pencil, charcoal, chalk, and conté crayon are familiar media to art students. Being soft mediums they are capable of providing (if desired) very gradual changes of dark to light. The Prud'hon drawing **(A)** shows the subtle and gradual transitions possible.

A medium such as black ink, by its nature, gives decidedly sharp value contrast. But this can be altered in several ways. The artist may use what is called **cross-hatching** (black lines of various densities that, seen against the white background, can give the impression of different grays). Again, variations are possible. These lines may be done with careful, repetitive precision (as seen in many drawings and etchings) or in a loose, freely spontaneous manner **(B)**. An artist may also choose the technique of **wash drawing,** in which the black ink is mixed with water, diluting the ink to produce desired shades of gray.

There are other possibilities. The van Gogh drawing **(C)** creates areas of gray by means of small strokes of the pen, repeated lines, and sometimes dots. These marks create a range of both values and textures.

The use of dots to create visual grays is a very common procedure, though we may not realize it. All of the black-and-white halftones we see daily in newspapers, books, and magazines are actually areas of tiny black dots in various concentrations to produce visual grays. This is a photomechanical process, but the same effect can be seen in Seurat's drawing **(D)**. Here the "dots" are created by the artist scraping a soft conté crayon over a heavily textured white paper. Again, dots of black produce visual grays.

With the same idea **E** presents a definite visual feeling of grays and, hence, dimension and volume. But this is a "drawing" done by a computer. The grays are actually created by the positioning of hundreds of tiny computer symbols of various densities that combine with the white background to give us the impression of many different grays.

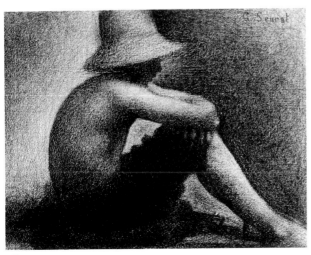

D

E

13

COLOR

INTRODUCTION

It is not only the professional artist or designer who deals with color. All of us make color decisions almost every day. We constantly choose items to purchase of which the color is a major factor. Our world today is marked by bold uses of color in every area of ordinary living. We can make color choices for everything from home appliances to bank checks—it seems that most things we use have blossomed out in bright colors. Fashion design, interior design, architecture, industrial design—all fields in art are now increasingly concerned with color.

Therefore everyone can profit by knowing some basic color principles. Unfortunately the study of color can be rather complex. The word color has so many aspects that it means different things to a physicist, optician, psychiatrist, poet, lighting engineer, and painter, and the analysis of color becomes a multifaceted report in which many experts competently describe their findings. Shelves of books in the library on the topic attest that comprehensive study of color from all viewpoints is impossible in a limited space.

However, any study of color must start with a few important, basic facts. The essential fact of color theory is that color is a property of light, not an object itself. This property of light was illustrated by Sir Isaac Newton in the seventeenth century, when he put white light through a prism. The prism broke up white light into the familiar rainbow of hues **(A)**. Objects have no color of their own but merely the ability to reflect certain rays of white light, which contain all the colors. Blue objects absorb all the rays except the blue ones, and these are reflected to our eyes. Black objects absorb all the rays; white objects reflect all of them. The significance of this fact for the artist is that as light changes, color will change.

But although color indeed comes from light, the guidelines of color mixing and usage are different depending on whether the color source is light or pigments and dyes. Rays of light are direct light, whereas the color of paint is reflected light. Color from light combines and forms new visual sensations based on what is called the **additive system.** On the other hand, pigments combine in the **subtractive system.** This term is appropriate. Blue paint is ''blue'' because when light hits its surface the pigment absorbs (or ''subtracts'') all of the color components except the blue that is reflected to our eyes. Artists should be aware of both systems. The painter, of course, will be mainly concerned with the subtractive, whereas the stage lighting designer, photographer, and often the interior designer will be concerned with the additive.

Lights projected from different sources mix according to the additive method. The diagram in **B** shows the three **primary colors** of light—red, green, and blue—and the colors produced where two hues overlap. The three primaries combined will produce white light. **Complementary** (or opposite) hues in light (red/cyan, blue/yellow, green/magenta) when mixed will again produce an **achromatic (neutral)** gray or white. Where light from a cyan (blue-green) spotlight and from a separate red spotlight overlap, the visual sensation is basically white. Combining these two colors in paint would produce a dark neutral ''mud''—anything but white.

This latter mixture of pigments functions according to the subtractive system. The red paint reflects little or no blue-green, and the blue-green paint reflects little or no red. When mixed together they act like two filters which now combine to reflect less light, thus approaching black (or a dark neutral) as the result. All paint mixture is to some degree subtractive; that is, the mixture is always weaker than at least one of the parent colors.

Because this book aims primarily at use in studio art classes, where the usual medium is paint, the information in this section refers mainly to the subtractive system of color usage.

A

A The spectrum of colors is created by passing white
light through a prism.
B Colors of light mix according to the additive process.

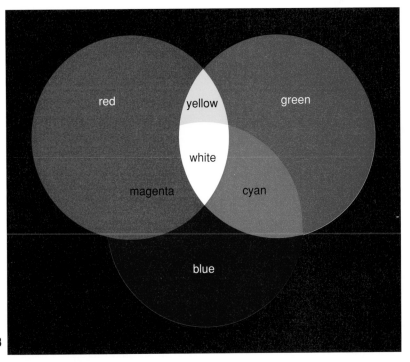

B

A Claude Monet. *London, The Houses of Parliament: Stormy Sky.* 1904. Oil on canvas, 32⅛ × 36¼″ (82 × 92 cm). Musée des Beaux-Arts, Lille.

B Claude Monet. *London, The Houses of Parliament: Sun Breaking Through the Fog.* 1904. Oil on canvas, 31⅞ × 36¼″ (81 × 92 cm). Musée d'Orsay, Paris.

C The red-purple squares, although seemingly different, are identical.

D A brilliant, vibrant color will not show much change despite different surroundings.

COLOR CHARACTERISTICS

Color theory is an extremely complex science. Although study of such factors as the various light wavelengths of different colors and the color/heat relationship is interesting, it is complicated and goes beyond our concern here.

Color has a basic, instinctive, visual appeal. Great art has been created in black and white, but few artists have totally ignored the added visual interest that color lends. The uninhibited use of color has been a primary characteristic of art in this century. Some artists use color primarily as an emotional element, and many artists use color in a strictly intuitive way. However, there have been artists who studied color per se and thereby have added immeasurably to our knowledge of color and color usage. Today's artists and students (and authors) owe a great debt to the twentieth-century artist Josef Albers, who as a painter and teacher has devoted a career to the study of color and color relationships. His books and paintings have contributed invaluably to our knowledge of color. Many of the concepts in this discussion are reflections of his research and teaching.

Color is a product of light. Therefore as light changes, the color we observe will change. What color is grass? Green? Grass may be almost gray at dawn, yellow-green at noon, and blue-black at midnight. The colors of things are constantly changing with the light. Though this is a simple visual fact, there is also the factor of the color constancy effect, which is our mind insisting that the grass is green despite the visual evidence to the contrary. This constancy effect is actually useful from the standpoint of human adaptation and survival. Imagine the problems if we questioned the colors of things with each new perception. Yet it is just this kind of questioning that has led artists such as Monet to reveal the range of color sensations around us. Monet's two paintings of the Houses of Parliament shown in **A** and **B** are typical of this artist's reinvestigation of the same setting under different circumstances of light. The titles of *Stormy Sky* (**A**) and *Sun Breaking Through the Fog* (**B**) give an insight into the situations that stimulated paintings with similar compositions but vastly different color relationships.

Related to the idea of color changing with the light, one other color phenomenon is important: our perception of colors changes according to their surroundings. Even in the same light, a color will appear different depending on the colors that are adjacent to it. Rarely do we see a color by itself. Normally colors are seen in conjunction with others and the visual differences are often amazing. A change in **value** (dark and light) is a common occurrence. Example **C** illustrates that even the color effect itself changes. The smaller "pink" squares are identical; the visual differences are caused by the various background colors these squares are placed against. In **D**, however, the two yellow areas, despite different background colors, still look about the same. With pure vibrant colors, optical changes will be very slight. Grayed, neutral colors are constantly changing in different contexts.

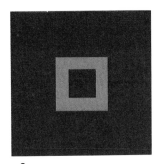   

C

D

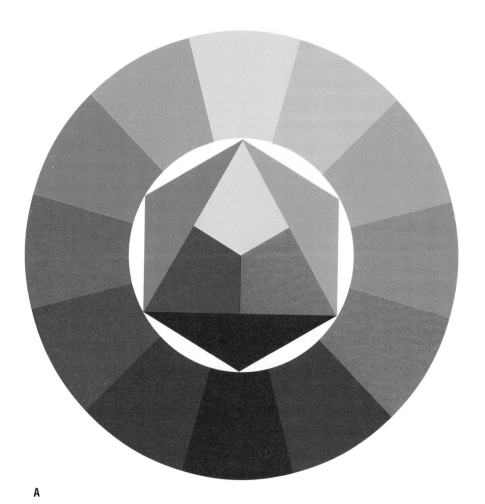

A

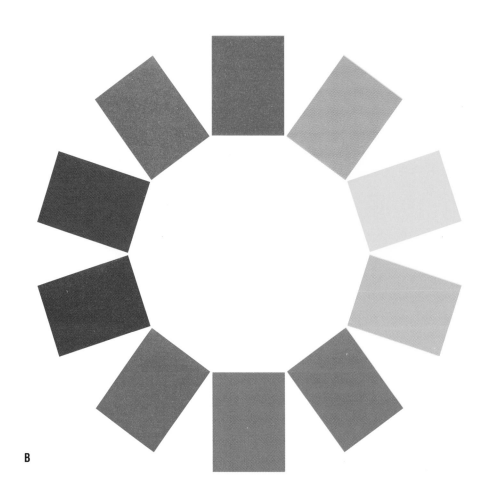

B

PROPERTIES OF COLOR

HUE

The first property of color is what we call **hue.** Hue simply refers to the name of the color. Red, orange, green, and purple are hues. Although the words *hue* and *color* are often used as synonyms, this is a bit confusing as there is a distinction between the two terms. The word hue describes the visual sensation of the different parts of the color spectrum. However, one hue can be varied to produce many colors. So even though there are relatively few hues, there can be an almost unlimited number of colors. Pink, rose, scarlet, maroon, and crimson are all colors, but the hue in each case is red. We are all aware that in the world of commercial products, color names abound; Plum, Adobe, Colonial Blue, Desert Sunset, Mayan Gold, and Avocado are a few examples. These often romantic images are extremely inexact terms that mean only what the manufacturers think they mean. The same hue (or color) can have dozens of different commercial names. You will even notice that the same hue can have different names in different color systems. "Blue," for instance, may be a blue-violet in one system and a cyan in another. One system may use the term "purple" and another "violet." Try to see past the names given to the colors and look instead at the relationships.

The most common organization for the relationships of the basic colors is the color wheel shown in **A**. The wheel system dates back to the early eighteenth century, and this version is one updated by Johannes Itten in this century. This particular organization uses twelve hues, which are divided into three categories.

The three **primary colors** are red, yellow, and blue. From these, all other colors can *theoretically* be mixed.

The three **secondary colors** are mixtures of the two primaries: Red and yellow make orange; yellow and blue make green; blue and red make violet.

The six **tertiary colors** are mixtures of a primary and an adjacent secondary: Blue and green make blue-green, red and violet make red-violet, and so on.

The color wheel of twelve hues is the one still in most common use. If you look closely, however, you will notice that the complements are not consistent with those shown in the illustration of additive and subtractive primaries. Furthermore, if you try mixing colors based on this wheel (such as blue and red to make violet), you will find the results to be dull and unsatisfactory. The color wheel shown in **B** is based on the **Munsell Color System,** and this version has ten equal visual steps. Mixtures of complements on this wheel will more closely produce neutrals (when tested as light mixtures on a computer, for example) and the positions of the colors are more useful in predicting paint mixtures as well.

A The twelve-step color wheel of Johannes Itten.
B A color wheel based on ten basic steps from the Munsell system. Courtesy of Macbeth, New Windsor, NY.

PROPERTIES OF COLOR

VALUE

The second property of color is **value,** which refers to the lightness or darkness of the hue. In pigment, value can be altered by adding white or black paint to the color. Adding white lightens the color and produces a **tint,** or high-value color. Adding black darkens the color and produces a **shade,** or low-value color. Individual perception varies, but most people can distinguish at least forty tints and shades of any color.

Not all the colors on the color wheel are shown at the same value. Each is shown at **normal value,** with the pure color unmixed and undiluted. The normal values of yellow and of blue, for example, are radically different **(A).** Because yellow is a light, or high-value, color, a yellow value scale shows many more shades than tints. The blue scale shows more tints, because normal blue is darker than middle value.

When working with paint and pigments the value of a color can also be altered by thinning the color with medium.

The more transparent color will be a lighter value when applied over a white background. The value of a color can also be altered by mixture with other hues: a naturally dark violet will darken a yellow, for example.

Value, like color itself, is variable and entirely dependent on surrounding hues for its visual sensation. In **B** the center green area appears much lighter and more luminous on the black background than on the white.

Colors changed by their context is a well-known occurrence. Amounts and repetition are also critical factors in color interaction. The same green shown in **B** takes on a different complexion when it is "woven" through the black or white as shown in **C.** In this case the white and green interact in a mixture effect, producing a lighter value field of color than the green and black pattern.

A

A Value scales for blue, gray, and yellow with equal visual steps.

B The same color will appear to change in value, depending upon the surrounding color.

C The visual mixture of green with black and white.

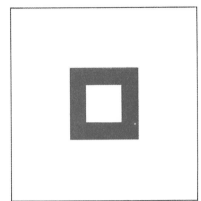

B

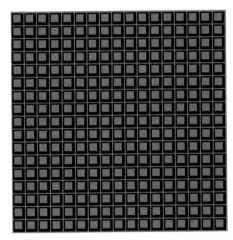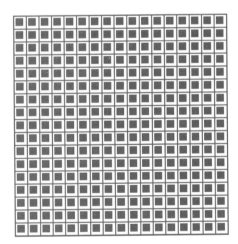

C

PROPERTIES OF COLOR

INTENSITY/COMPLEMENTARY COLORS

The third property of color is **intensity,** which refers to the brightness of a color. Because a color is at full intensity only when pure and unmixed, a relationship exists between *value* and *intensity*. Mixing black or white with a color changes its value but at the same time affects its intensity. To see the distinction between the two terms look at the two tints (high value) of red in example **A**. The tints have about the same degree of lightness, yet one might be called "rose," the other "shocking pink." The two colors are very different in their visual effect, and the difference comes from brightness or intensity. Intensity is sometimes called **chroma,** or **saturation.**

There are two ways to lower the intensity of a color, to make a color less bright, more neutral, and duller. One way is to mix gray with the color. Depending on the gray used, you can dull a color without changing its value. The second way is to mix a color with its **complement,** the color directly across from it on the color wheel. Example **B** shows an intensity scale involving the complementary colors blue and orange. Neutralized (low-intensity) versions of a color are often called **tones.** In **B** we see two intensity levels of blue and two intensity levels of orange with grey in the middle. As progressively more orange is added to the blue, the blue becomes duller, more grayed. The same is true of the orange, which becomes browner when blue is added.

Complementary colors are direct opposites in position and in character. Mixing complementary colors together neutralizes them, but when complementary colors are placed next to each other, they intensify each other's brightness. When blue and orange are side by side, each color will appear brighter than in any other context. This effect is called **simultaneous contrast,** meaning that each complement simultaneously intensifies the

visual brilliance of the other, so that the colors appear to vibrate. Artists use this visual effect when they wish to produce brilliant color.

Another phenomenon that defines complementary color is the **afterimage effect.** Stare at an area of intense color for a minute or so, and then glance away at a white piece of paper or wall. Suddenly an area of the complementary color will seem to appear. For example, when you look at the white wall after staring at a red shape, a definite blue-green area in somewhat the same shape will seem to take form on the wall.

Seldom will you find an artist using complementary contrast to the exclusion of other color relationships. De Kooning's *Pink Lady* **(C)** is vivid in the contrast between red and green, traditionally thought of as complementary colors. We know from the light primaries, however, that red and green are not exact complements, and their light mixture produces yellow (not a neutral). In fact, de Kooning seems to express this intuitively with the yellow shapes that surround the figure. Where the red and the green blend you can see the paint mixture is "olive" or a "dark yellow" produced by this subtractive mixture. The red and green are undeniably vibrant in their contrast due in part to their high intensity and similarity of value. In some areas (such as where the head rests on the hand) you can see that the artist pushed the green to the blue-green that is complementary to the red figure.

Pierre Bonnard uses complementary blue-violet and yellow in his painting shown in **D.** Not only do the colors vividly contrast with each other in juxtaposition, but neutral areas of the painting suggest a middle mixture between the two complements. Again the painting is not merely a complementary pairing, and the areas of pink offer a triadic third color to the composition.

SEE ALSO: *Color Symbolism, page 252.*

A

B

C

A Two tints of red at the same value have different intensities.

B One way to lower the intensity of a color is to mix it with its complement.

C Willem de Kooning. *Pink Lady.* Ca. 1944. Oil and charcoal on panel, 48¼ × 36¼″ (123 × 92 cm). Private collection.

D Pierre Bonnard. *Nude in the Bath.* 1936. Oil on canvas, 37 × 58″ (93 × 147 cm). Musée du Petit Palais, Paris.

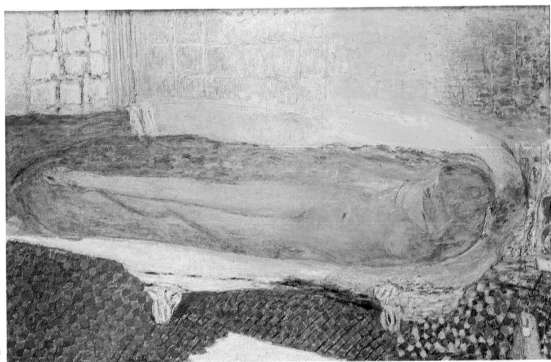

D

A

B

A Chuck Close. *Self Portrait*. 1986. Oil on canvas, 54½ × 42¼″ (138 × 107 cm). Courtesy of The Pace Gallery, New York.
B Workshop of Nicolas Bataille. *Arthur with Three Cardinals*, detail from the *Nine Heroes* series. Ca. 1385. Tapestry, 11′6½″ × 10′ (3.51 × 3.05 m). Metropolitan Museum of Art, New York (Cloisters Collection, Munsey Fund, 1932; 32.130.3a).
C Photograph with enlarged photomechanical dot pattern shows blending into different colors.

VISUAL COLOR MIXING

The mixing of pigments combines along certain guidelines to create new colors. However, muddy or dull colors are often the result. Even when mixing adjacent colors on the color wheel you may find the results to be less intense than you anticipated, and the farther apart the hues, the more subtractive (darker and duller) the mixture. To understand this process, think of the pigments as acting like filters, which in combination (or mixture) allow less light or color to reflect back off the colored surface to the viewer's eye.

Pigment simply will never reproduce the luminous and brilliant quality of light. Recognizing this, artists have struggled with the problem and tried various techniques to overcome it. One attempt is what is called **visual mixing.** Rather than mixing two colors on the palette, artists place two pure colors side by side in small areas so the viewer's eye (at a certain distance) will do the mixing. Or perhaps they drag a brush of thick pigment of one color loosely across a field of another color. The uneven paint application allows bits and pieces of the background to show through. Again the pure colors are mixed in our perception, not on the canvas.

Visual mixing is often associated with the Post-Impressionist era of the late nineteenth century and can be observed in the works of artists such as Seurat and van Gogh. The techniques of **pointillism** and **divisionism** both used small bits of juxtaposed color to produce different color sensations. In a way these artists anticipated the truly additive color mixing that occurs on a color television screen. This screen is composed of thousands of luminous pixels. The colors we see are a visual mix of the light primaries, red, blue, and green.

Such luminosity is not possible with the surface of painting. Still, artists continue to explore the possibilities of visual mixture, as can be seen in *Self Portrait* **(A)** by the contemporary painter Chuck Close. The large scale of this portrait assures that we will always be aware of the pattern of color bits and that they will not absolutely merge into a mixture. In fact, this technique is usually most luminous when this is the case.

The basic idea of visual mixing is used in many areas. In creating mosaics, stirring up a bowl of red and blue tiles will not, of course, produce purple tesserae. Instead, small pieces of pure-colored tiles are interspersed to produce the effect of many other intermediate colors. The same process is employed in creating tapestries. Weavers working with a limited number of colored yarns or threads can intermingle them, so that at at distance the eye merges them and creates an impression of many hues and values **(B)**. A more everyday example is plaid or tartan fabric. From a distance the material can seem to be a pattern of many colors and values. Close inspection might reveal that just two or three colored threads have been woven in various densities to produce all the visual variations.

A version of the pointillist technique is now used every day in a photomechanical adaptation in the printing of color pictures. The numerous colors we see in printed reproductions usually are all produced by just four basic colors in a small dot pattern. The dots in this case are so tiny that we are totally unaware of them unless we use a magnifying glass to visually enlarge them **(C)**.

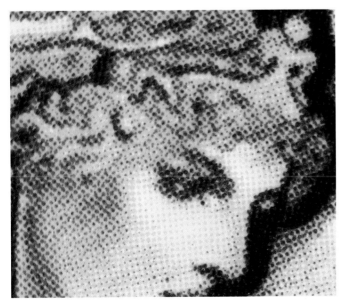

C

A

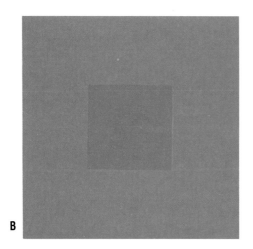

B

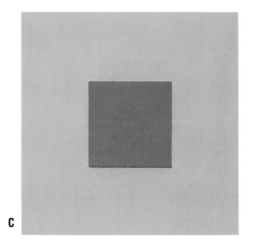

C

COOL/WARM COLORS

Cool colors? Warm colors? These may seem odd adjectives to apply to the visual sensation of color, as "cool" and "warm" are sensations of touch, not sight. Nevertheless, we are all familiar with the terms and continually refer to colors this way. Because of the learned association of color and objects, we continue to identify and relate the sensations of the different senses. Hence, red and orange (fire) and yellow (sunlight) become identified as warm colors. Similarly, blue (sky, water) and green (grass, plants) are always thought of as cool colors.

Touching an area of red will assuredly not burn your hand, but *looking* at red will indeed induce a feeling of warmth. The effect may be purely psychological, but the results are very real. We have all read of the workers in an office painted blue complaining of the chill and actually getting colds. The problem was solved not by raising the thermostat but by repainting the office in warm tones of brown. The painting by Georgia O'Keeffe in **A** makes us truly feel the cool, misty atmosphere of a mountain lake by her emphasis on the blue side of the spectrum.

We generally think of the colors yellow through red-violet as the warm side of the color wheel and yellow-green through violet as the cool segment. The visual effects are quite variable, however, and again depend a great deal on the context in which we see the color. In **B** the green square appears very warm surrounded by a background of blue. But in **C** the identical green, when placed on an orange background, shifts and becomes a cooler tone.

As warm colors tend to advance, while cool colors seem to recede, the artist may use the warm/cool relationship to establish a feeling of depth and volume. Probably no group of artists has investigated and expanded our ideas of color more than the Impressionists. The blue and purple shadows (instead of gray and black) that so shocked the nineteenth-century public seem to us today perfectly logical and reasonable. In Sargent's watercolor painting *Reading* **(D)** notice how the folds of the "white" dress are molded by the artist's use of warm and cool contrasts. The highlights in warm tones gradually change to cooler colors expressing the shadow areas.

A Georgia O'Keeffe. *Lake George.* 1922. Oil on canvas, 16¼ × 22″ (41.2 × 56 cm). San Francisco Museum of Modern Art (gift of Charlotte Mack).
B A colored area on a cool background will appear warmer in tone.
C The same color surrounded by a warm background seems cool.
D John Singer Sargent. *Simplon Pass: Reading.* 1911. Watercolor on paper, 20 × 14″ (51 × 36 cm). Museum of Fine Arts, Boston (The Hayden Collection. Charles Henry Hayden Fund).

D

COLOR AS EMPHASIS

Areas of emphasis in a work of art create visual interest and, naturally, have been carefully planned by the artist. Color is very often the means chosen to provide this emphasis—color is probably the most direct device to use. When planning emphasis, we might think of using a larger size somewhere, or perhaps a change in shape, or isolating one element by itself. As can be seen by the diagrams in **A**, the use of color will dominate over these other devices. You will notice that the accented color is not a radically different hue or very different in value or intensity. Such contrasts, of course, would heighten the effect. But **A** shows that color by its very character commands attention.

Sometimes the artist may wish to create a definite focal point or center of attention that the observer will see first. A bright or vivid color, such as the patch of orange in Elmer Bischoff's *Orange Sweater* **(B)**, immediately will attract our eye. The orange sweater is echoed by weaker oranges and yellows elsewhere in the painting, but is clearly a focal point by color and placement.

In Gérôme's painting **(C)** the brightest hues are used to emphasize the costumed figure attending to the dying Pierot. The red costume serves to call attention to the red blood stain on Pierot's white chest. By contrast the rest of the painting is virtually colorless, and even Harlequin's bright costume has been subdued to low intensities.

A Color is so strong a visual element that it will dominate other devices to establish emphasis.

B Elmer Bischoff. *Orange Sweater.* 1955. Oil on canvas, 48½ × 57″ (123.2 × 148.8 cm). San Francisco Museum of Modern Art (gift of Mr. and Mrs. Mark Schorer).

C Jean Léon Gérôme. *The Duel after the Masquerade.* Ca. 1857. Oil on canvas, 15⅜ × 22⅛″ (39 × 56 cm). Walters Art Gallery, Baltimore.

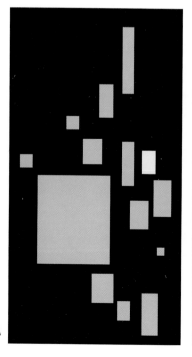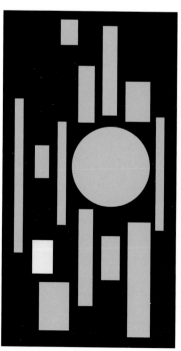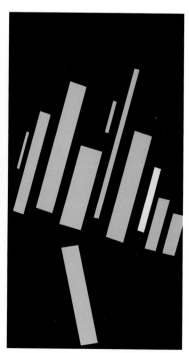

A

B

C

COLOR AND BALANCE

Unlike symmetrical balance, asymmetry is based on the concept of using differing objects on either side of the center axis. But to create visual balance, the objects must have equal weight or attraction. Color is often used to achieve this effect.

A comparison of **A** and **B** will illustrate the idea. In **A** Joan Miró's painting is shown just in black and white. From this reproduction, the composition might appear off balance. The left side, with the contrasting white circle and solid black triangle and notched rectangle, seems to have more visual interest than the right side where there is less delineation of the shapes and little value contrast. But when the same painting is seen in color **(B)**, the balance is immediately clear. A circular shape on the right is actually a brilliant red in color. This very vivid color note in a predominantly neutral painting attracts our eye and can balance the elements on the left.

The use of color to balance a composition is very common and seen in many different periods and different styles of art.

Wayne Thiebaud's *Rabbit* **(C)** is at first glance the simplest of compositions: a white rabbit placed in the center of a white field. The rabbit's head is the natural focus of the composition, and this directs our attention to the left side of the painting. The intense blue shadow on the right-hand side of the composition provides the balance.

The painting by Paul Gauguin shown in **D** is virtually split in half, with almost colorless figures the focus on the left side. Figures are a natural subject of interest and curiosity for a viewer. Here they are emphasized primarily by the value contrast of their pale skin tones against the unusual dark shapes created by their clothing. A balancing area of interest is created by the twin orange tree trunks and vivid red fence that dominate the right half of the composition.

A

B

C

A Joan Miró. *The Birth of the World*. 1925. Oil on
   canvas, 8′2¾″ × 6′6¾″ (2.5 × 2.0 m). The Museum
   of Modern Art, New York (acquired through an
   anonymous fund, the Mr. and Mrs. Joseph Slifka and
   Armand G. Erpf funds and by gift of the artist).

B Seeing *A* in color shows us how color achieves the
   balance.

C Wayne Thiebaud. *Rabbit*. 1966. Pastel on paper,
   14¾ × 19½″ (37 × 50 cm). Courtesy, Collection Mrs.
   Edwin A. Bergman and the artist.

D Paul Gauguin. *Old Women at Arles*. 1888. Oil on
   canvas, 29 × 36″ (73 × 92 cm). Photograph © 1993,
   The Art Institute of Chicago (Mr. and Mrs. Lewis
   Larned Coburn Memorial Collection, 1934.391). All
   rights reserved.

D

COLOR AND SPACE

There is a direct relationship between color and a visual impression of depth, or pictorial space. Colors have an innate advancing or receding quality because of slight muscular reactions in our eyes as we focus on different colors. Intense, warm colors (red, orange, yellow) seem to come forward; cool colors (blue, green) seem to go back. The design of numbers in various colors (A) illustrates this principle. When we look at this design we can see that some numbers immediately "pop" forward and actually seem closer than others. Some numbers seem to stay back, with others seeming to be far in the background. Relative size can influence this effect, with larger items automatically seeming closer. But notice that size is not really a consideration here. There are numbers of equal size and weight that advance or recede based solely on their color.

Another aspect of the relationship of color and spatial illusion is that the dust in the earth's atmosphere breaks up the color rays from distant objects and makes them appear bluish. As objects recede, any brilliance of color becomes more neutral, finally seeming to be gray-blue.

Artists can use color's spatial properties to create either an illusion of depth or a flat, two-dimensional pattern. The landscape in B gives a feeling of great distance. The overlapping planes of the receding canyon walls change in color and value. The artist has concentrated warm browns and oranges in the close foreground. Then, as distance increases, the elements become grayer, cooler, and more bluish in color.

In contrast, Derain in his landscape (C) consciously flattens and compresses space by his use of color. Some of the foreground tree trunks are an advancing red, but now the background hills are a brilliant advancing orange that comes forward and denies the implicit depth of the scene. A colorful and decorative, but relatively flat, painting results.

Color values are also important in spatial illusion. Whatever the colors used, high contrast comes forward visually, whereas areas of lesser contrast generally recede. Examples A and B show this effect. The dark-colored numbers in A generally stay back, being close in value to the black background. The value-contrasting light yellows come forward. In B the distant patterns of light and shadow are less pronounced than the strong contrast of light and dark in the foreground.

A   Advertisement with Electric Calculator Symbols.
    Reprinted with permission: Ing. C. Olivetti & C.,
    S.p.A.; G. Pintori, Artist.
B   George Gardner Symons. *Grand Canyon, Arizona.*
    Ca. 1914. Oil on canvas, 47 × 71″ (119 × 180 cm).
    Collection J. C. Penney Company.
C   Andre Derain. *Landscape.* Ca. 1905–06. Oil on
    canvas mounted on board, 20 × 25½″ (50.8 × 64.8
    cm). San Francisco Museum of Modern Art (bequest
    of Harriet Lane Levy).

A

B

C

COLOR SCHEMES

MONOCHROMATIC, ANALOGOUS, COMPLEMENTARY, TRIADIC

There are four basic color schemes (or **color harmonies,** as they are often called).

A **monochromatic** color scheme involves the use of only one hue. The hue can vary in value, and pure black or white may be added. Painter Mark Tansey has varied the values in **A** by a process of wiping away the paint to reveal the white "ground" underneath. The use of monochrome unites the montage of images that come together in this painting. Tansey also uses monochrome as a way to emphasize textural difference over color difference and to suggest the qualities of an old photograph.

An **analogous** color scheme combines several hues that sit next to each other on the color wheel. Again, the hues may vary in value. The Navajo textile **(B)** shows the related, harmonious feeling that analogous color lends to a design. This blanket includes colors adjacent to red on the color wheel.

A **complementary** color scheme, as the term implies, joins colors opposite each other on the color wheel. This combination will produce a sense of contrast even when one of the hues is a lower intensity, as in Hohenstein's poster for *Tosca* **(C)**.

A **split complementary** color scheme is related to the complementary scheme, but would employ colors adjacent to one of the complementary pairs. For example a red might be balanced by a blue and a green in place of the complementary blue-green.

A **triadic** color scheme involves three hues equally spaced on the color wheel. Red, yellow, and blue would be the most common example **(D)**. Because the hues come from different parts of the wheel, the result is lively.

These color schemes are probably more applicable to such design areas as interiors, posters, and packaging than to painting. In painting, color often is used intuitively, and many artists would reject the idea that they work by formula. But knowing these harmonies can help designers consciously to plan the visual effects they want a finished pattern to have. Moreover, color can easily provide a visual unity that might not be obvious in the initial pattern of shapes. Even though design aims vary, often the more complicated and "busy" the pattern of shapes is, the more useful will be a strict control of the color, and the reverse is also true.

Color unity is described by another term. We often speak of the **tonality** of a design or painting. Tonality refers to the dominance of a single color or the visual importance of a hue that seems to pervade the whole color structure despite the presence of other colors. Monochromatic patterns (as value studies in one color) give a uniform tonality, because only one hue is present. Analogous color schemes can also produce a dominant tonality, as **B** shows. When colors are chosen from one part of the color wheel, they will share one hue in common. In **B** the red, orange, and brown all derive from red, and so yield a red tonality.

A

B

A Mark Tansey. *Forward Retreat*. 1986. Oil on canvas, 94 × 116″ (2.4 × 2.9 m). Courtesy of Eli Broad Family Foundation, Santa Monica, CA.

B Navaho blanket/rug. Ca. 1885–95. 55 × 82″ (140.5 × 207.8 cm). Natural History Museum of Los Angeles County (William Randolph Hearst Collection, A.5141.42–153).

C Adolfo Hohenstein. Poster for *Tosca*. 1899. Poster Photo Archives, Posters Please, Inc., New York.

D Charles Demuth. *Buildings Abstraction, Lancaster, 1931*. 1931. Oil on panel, 27⅞ × 23⅝″ (71 × 60 cm). © The Detroit Institute of Arts (Founders Society purchase, General Membership Fund).

D

C

A

B

C

D

COLOR DISCORD AND VIBRATING COLORS

Color discord is the opposite of color harmony. A combination of discordant colors can be visually disturbing. Discordant colors have no basic affinity for each other (as you would find with analogous colors), nor do they seem to balance each other (as with a complementary contrast).

The term "discord" conveys an immediate negative impression. Discord in life, in a personal relationship, may not be pleasant, but it often provides a stimulus or excitement. In the same manner, discord can be extremely useful in art and design.

Mild discord results in exciting, eye-catching color combinations. The world of fashion has exploited the idea to the point that mildly discordant combinations are almost commonplace. A discordant color note in a painting or design may contribute visual surprise and also may better express certain themes or ideas. A poster may better attract attention by its startling colors.

Once rules were taught about just which color combinations were harmonious and which were definitely to be avoided because the colors did not "go together." A combination of pink and orange was unthinkable; even blue and green patterns were suspect. Today these rules seem silly, and we approach color more freely, seeking unexpected combinations.

The color pair of orange and red-purple shown in **A** is one that has been called discordant. This is typical of color pairings that are widely separated on the color wheel but not complements. In **B** the effect is even more discordant when the red-purple is lightened to the same value as the orange.

A painting by Archibald Motley **(C)** takes full advantage of this red-purple and orange color pairing to capture the festive atmosphere of a nighttime barbecue. The colors conjure the flavor and atmosphere of the setting.

Certain color pairings are almost difficult to look at. In fact our eye experiences a conflict in trying to perceive them simultaneously. Red and cyan will literally have a vibrating edge when their values are equal and their intensities are high **(D)**. You will find this to be true for a range of colors when they are paired at equal value, but the effect is strongest with reds opposed to blues and greens. Nancy Crow exploits this almost electric effect in her quilt shown in **E**.

A Pure orange and red-purple.
B The same colors with closer values.
C Archibald J. Motley, Jr. *Barbecue.* 1934. Oil on canvas, 36¼ × 40⅛" (92 × 102 cm). The Howard University Gallery of Art, Washington, DC.
D Red and cyan will have a vibrating edge when values are equal and intensities are high.
E Nancy Crow. *Color Blocks #18.* 1992. Quilt, hand-dyed cottons, 49 × 32" (125 × 81 cm). © Nancy Crow, 1992.

E

COLOR USES

LOCAL, OPTICAL, ARBITRARY

There are three basic ways in which color can be used in painting. An artist may use what is called **local color.** This term refers to the identifying color of an object under ordinary daylight. Local color is the objective color that we ''know'' objects are: grass is green, bananas are yellow, apples are red. The use of local color reinforces, or takes advantage of our preconceptions of an object's color.

Visually, the red of an apple can change radically, depending on the illumination. Because color is a property of light, the color of any object changes at sunset, under moonlight, or by candlelight as in **A**. Even atmospheric effects can visually change the local color of distant objects, such as faraway mountains appearing blue. An artist reproducing these visual effects is using **optical color.**

In **arbitrary color,** the color choices are subjective, rather than based on the colors seen in nature. The artist's colors are selected for design, aesthetic, or emotional reasons. Large patches of intense color frame the head in *Mme. Matisse/The Green Line* (**B**), and the green line referred to in the title is a bold subjective color choice. Arbitrary color is sometimes difficult to pinpoint, because many painters take some artistic liberties in using color. Has the artist disregarded the colors he saw or has he merely intensified and exaggerated the visual reference? This latter use is termed **heightened color.** Wolf Kahn's painting shown in **C** intensifies the red earthen pathway in the warm sunlight, and the intensified violet emphasizes the cool shadows and water beneath the trees.

Pure arbitrary (or subjective) color is often seen in twentieth-century painting. Just as art in general has moved away from naturalism, so has arbitrary color tended to become an important interest. Even color photography—with filters, infrared film, and various darkroom techniques—has experimented widely in the area of unexpected color effects.

These categories of color use obviously apply to paintings with identifiable subject matter. In nonobjective art the forms have no apparent reference to natural objects, so that the color is also nonobjective. Purely aesthetic considerations determine the color choices.

A

B

A Georges de la Tour. *The Repentant Magdalene.* Ca. 1640. Oil on canvas, 44½ × 36½″ (113 × 93 cm). © National Gallery of Art, Washington, DC (Ailsa Mellon Bruce Fund).
B Henri Matisse. *Portrait of Mme. Matisse/The Green Line.* 1905. Oil on canvas, 16 × 12⅞″ (40.5 × 32.5 cm). Statens Museum for Kunst, Copenhagen.
C Wolf Kahn. *Receding Towpath II.* 1986. Oil on canvas, 53¼ × 53¼″ (135 × 135 cm). The Gerald Peters Gallery, Santa Fe, NM.

C

A

B

EMOTIONAL COLOR

*"Ever since our argument, I've been **blue**."*

*"I saw **red** when she lied to me."*

*"You're certainly in a **black** mood today."*

*"I was **green** with envy when I saw their new house."*

These statements are emotional. The speakers are expressing an emotional reaction, and somehow a color reference makes the meaning clearer, because color appeals to our emotions and feelings. For artists who wish to arouse an emotional response in the viewer, color is the most effective element. Even before we "read" the subject matter or identify the forms, the color creates an atmosphere to which we respond.

In a very basic instance, we commonly recognize so-called warm and cool colors. Yellows, oranges, and reds give us an instinctive feeling of warmth and evoke warm, happy, cheerful reactions. Cooler blues and greens are automatically associated with quieter, less outgoing feelings and can express melancholy **(A)** or depression. These examples are generalities, of course, for the combination of colors is vital, and the artist can also influence our reactions by the values and intensities of the colors selected.

Paintings in which color causes an emotional reaction and relates to the thematic subject matter are very common. The flat red background in Leon Golub's *Mercenaries IV* **(B)** is evocative of blood and impending violence associated with the threatening image of the mercenaries. The intense red seems to push these figures at us, heightening our emotional response to the subject matter.

With a change of context the same hue can evoke a different response. Red is also a dominant color in Hans Hofmann's *Golden Wall* **(C)**, and once again the red seems to push the other shapes toward us. The nonobjective shapes of intense color and modulations in the red field create a vibrant, joyous quality in this painting quite different from Golub's *Mercenaries IV*.

The power of color to evoke an emotional response is undeniable. The context or situation the artist creates in a composition determines whether the effect is inventive or merely a cliché.

A Pablo Picasso. *Crouching Woman.* 1902. Oil on canvas, 35 × 28″ (90 × 71 cm). Staatsgalerie, Stuttgart.

B Leon Golub. *Mercenaries IV.* 1980. Acrylic on linen, 120 × 230½″ (3 × 6 m). Private collection, courtesy of the artist.

C Hans Hofmann. *The Golden Wall.* 1961. Oil on canvas, 5′ × 6′½″ (1.51 × 1.82 m). Photograph © 1993, The Art Institute of Chicago (Mr. and Mrs. Frank G. Logan Prize Fund, 1962.775). All rights reserved.

C

COLOR SYMBOLISM

*"Don't worry, he's true **blue**."*

*"I caught him **red**-handed."*

*"So I told her a little **white** lie."*

*"Why not just admit you're too **yellow** to do it?"*

We frequently utter statements that employ color references to describe character traits or human behavior. These color references are **symbolic.** The colors in the above statements symbolize abstract concepts or ideas: fidelity, sin, innocence, and cowardice. The colors do not stand for tangibles like fire, grass, water, or even sunlight. They represent mental, conceptual qualities. The colors chosen to symbolize various ideas are often arbitrary, or the initial reasons for their choice have become so deeply buried in history we no longer remember them. Can we really explain why green means "go" and red signifies "stop"?

A main point to remember is that symbolic color references are cultural: They are not worldwide but vary from one society to another. What is the color of mourning that one associates with a funeral? Our reply might be black, but the answer would be white in India, violet in Turkey, brown in Ethiopia, and yellow in Burma. What is the color of royalty? We think of purple (dating back to the Egyptians), but the royal color was yellow in dynastic China and red in ancient Rome (a custom continued today in the cardinals' robes of the Catholic Church). What does a bride wear? White is our response, but yellow is the choice in Hindu India and red in China.

Different eras and different cultures invent different color symbols. The symbolic use of color was very important in ancient art for identifying specific figures or deities to an illiterate public. Not only the ancients used color in this manner—in the countless pictures of the Virgin Mary through centuries of Western art, she is almost always shown in a blue robe over a red or white dress.

Symbolic color designations are less important in art than they once were. Perhaps we are more conscious today of symbolic color as it is used in advertising, such as green to evoke an association with environmental responsibility, or black to connote sophistication. Until recently black was a taboo for food packaging: now it may suggest a premium product.

Jasper Johns' flag image shown in **A** startles us with the "wrong colors." Red, white, and blue are replaced with green, black, and orange. On one level this is a simple optical trick. The afterimage of this flag is meant to produce the "true" colors in the space below.

More powerful than this illusion is the recognition of how strongly Americans associate red, white, and blue with patriotic themes, and how the Johns' variation disrupts or disturbs our expectations for the image.

A Jasper Johns. *Flag*. 1968. Lithograph, printed in color, composition: 34⅝ × 25⅞" (88 × 66 cm). The Museum of Modern Art, New York (gift of the Celeste and Armand Bartos Foundation).

A

COLOR VERSUS VALUE

We customarily think of an artist as working with color, but consider the vast area of drawings, prints, and photographs produced using pure value and no color. Also consider fields such as sculpture and architecture. Here, though color is present, the main design consideration has often been value because of the usual monotone of the materials involved. Texture, which is so important an element in these fields, is essentially a variation in light and dark visual patterns. It would seem that an artist in almost any field or specialization should be skillful in manipulating both color and value.

Do color and value work together or at cross-purposes? This question has been argued over the centuries. Some critics have maintained that the emphasis in a work should be on one *or* the other. Some artists of the past seem to have thought this way also. Leonardo da Vinci called color the "greatest enemy of art," and Titian supposedly said that an artist needs only three colors. Obviously, these artists emphasized value changes, rather than contrast of pure color. The Fauves and Expressionists of the twentieth century would undoubtedly agree with van Gogh's statement, "Coloring is what makes a painter a painter."

Historically it seems that, for whatever reason, many artists have often chosen to put the emphasis on either color or value. Art historians outlining the stylistic changes in art have described shifts in this area as indicative of a new period.

This changing of color/value emphasis among different artists and different periods would explain why some works seem so inadequate when shown in a black-and-white illustration. While a Renaissance painting may be satisfactory, if not satisfying, shown only in value, a book on Impressionism would be impossible without any illustrations in color. The sparkle and brilliance of the original paintings would be lost.

A comparison between a black-and-white reproduction and a color one can be useful in revealing the relationship between the value structure and the color structure of a composition. The value structure of Stuart Davis' *Rapt at Rappaport's* **(A)** shows a fairly lively composition with light and dark shapes scattered like confetti across a gray field. When we see the same painting reproduced in color **(B)**, letters and shapes appear that are missing in the black-and-white version **(A)**. This is due to equal value relationships among the intense red, blue, and green.

A Stuart Davis. *Rapt at Rappaport's*. 1952. Oil on
B canvas, 52 × 40″ (131.8 × 101.4 cm). Hirshhorn Museum and Sculpture Garden, Smithsonian Institution (gift of the Joseph H. Hirshhorn Foundation, 1966).

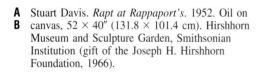

A

B

GLOSSARY

BY SEAN FOLEY

ABSTRACTION A visual representation that may have little resemblance to the real world. Abstraction can occur through a process of simplification or distortion in an attempt to communicate an essential aspect of a form or concept.

ACHROMATIC Black, gray, or white with no distinctive hues.

ADDITIVE SYSTEM A color mixing system in which combinations of different wavelengths of light create visual sensations of color.

AERIAL PERSPECTIVE The perception of less distinct contours and value contrasts as forms recede into the background. Colors appear to be washed out in the distance or take on the color of the atmosphere.

AESTHETICS A branch of philosophy concerned with the beautiful in art and how it is experienced by the viewer.

AFTERIMAGE Occurs after staring at an area of intense color for a certain amount of time and then quickly glancing away towards a white surface where the complementary color seems to appear.

ALLOVER PATTERN A composition that distributes emphasis uniformly throughout the two-dimensional surface by repetition of similar elements.

ALTERNATING RHYTHM A rhythm that consists of successive patterns in which the same elements reappear in a regular order. The motifs alternate consistently with one another to produce a regular (and anticipated) sequence.

AMBIGUITY Obscurity of motif or meaning.

AMPLIFIED PERSPECTIVE A dynamic and dramatic illusionistic effect created when the object is pointed directly at the viewer.

ANALOGOUS COLORS A color scheme that combines several hues located next to each other on the color wheel.

ANTICIPATED MOVEMENT The implication of movement on a two-dimensional surface caused by the viewer's past experience with a similar situation.

ART DECO A decorative style, popular in the 1920s, characterized by its geometric patterns and reflecting the rise of industry and mass production in the early twentieth century.

ASYMMETRICAL BALANCE Balance achieved with dissimilar objects that have equal visual weight or equal eye attraction.

AXIS A line of reference around which a form or composition is balanced.

BALANCE The equilibrium of opposing or interacting forces in a pictorial composition.

BIOMORPHIC Shapes derived from organic or natural forms.

BLURRED OUTLINE A visual device in which most details and the edges of a form are lost in the rapidity of the movement.

CALLIGRAPHIC Elegant, flowing lines suggestive of writing with an aesthetic value separate from its textual content.

CHIAROSCURO The use of light and dark values to imply depth and volume in a two-dimensional work of art.

CHROMA See Intensity.

CHROMATIC Relating to the hue or saturation of color.

CLASSICAL Suggestive of Greek and Roman ideals of beauty and purity of form, style, or technique.

CLOSED FORM The placement of objects in which the focal point of a composition keeps the viewer's attention within the picture.

COLLAGE An artwork created by assembling and pasting a variety of materials to a two-dimensional surface.

COLOR CONSTANCY A psychological compensation for changes in light when observing a color. A viewer interprets the color to be the same under various light conditions.

COLOR DISCORD A perception of dissonance in a color relationship.

COLOR HARMONY Any one of a number of color relationships based on groupings within the color wheel (See Analogous Colors, Color Triad, and Complementary).

COLOR SYMBOLISM Employing color to signify human character traits or concepts.

COLOR TRIAD Three colors equidistant on the color wheel.

COLOR WHEEL An arrangement of colors based on the sequence of hues in the visible spectrum.

COMPLEMENTARY A color scheme incorporating opposite hues on the color wheel. Complementary colors accentuate each other in juxtaposition, and neutralize each other in mixture.

COMPOSITION The overall arrangement and organization of visual elements on the two-dimensional surface.

CONCEPTUAL Artwork based on an idea. An art movement in which the idea is more important than the two- or three-dimensional artwork.

CONTENT An idea conveyed through the artwork that implies the subject matter, story, or information the artist communicates to the viewer.

CONTINUATION A line or edge that continues from one form to the next allowing the eye to move smoothly from one form to the next through a composition.

CONTINUITY The visual relationship between two or more individual designs.

CONTOUR A line used to follow the edges of forms and thus describe their outlines.

COOL COLOR A color closer to blue on the color wheel.

CROSSHATCHING A drawing technique in which a series of parallel lines are layered over each other to build up value and to define form and volume.

CRYSTALLOGRAPHIC BALANCE Balance with equal emphasis over an entire two-dimensional surface, so that there is always the same visual weight or attraction wherever you may look. Also called Allover Pattern.

CURVILINEAR Rounded and curving forms which tend to imply soft flowing shapes and compositions.

DESIGN A planned arrangement of visual elements in order to construct an organized visual pattern.

DISTORTION A departure from an accepted perception of a form or object to convey a different visual experience. Distortion often manipulates established proportional standards.

DRAFTSMANSHIP The quality of drawing or rendering.

EARTHWORKS Artworks created by altering a large area of land using natural and organic materials. Earthworks are usually large scale projects that take formal advantage of space available.

EMOTIONAL COLOR A subjective approach to color usage to elicit an emotional response in the viewer.

ENIGMATIC Puzzling or cryptic in appearance or meaning.

EQUILIBRIUM Visual balance between opposing compositional elements.

EQUIVOCAL SPACE An ambiguous space in which it is hard to distinguish the foreground from the background. Your perception seems to flip-flop.

EXPRESSIONISM An artistic style in which an emotion is more important than adherence to any perceptual realism. It is characterized by the exaggeration and distortion of objects in order to evoke an emotional response from the viewer.

FACADE The face or frontal aspect of a form.

FAUVE A French term meaning ''wild beasts'' and descriptive of an artistic style characterized by the use of bright and intense expressionist color schemes.

FIGURE Any positive shape or form noticeably separated from the background or, negative space.

FOCAL POINT A compositional device emphasizing a certain area or object to draw attention to the piece and to encourage closer scrutiny of the work.

FORM When referring to objects, it is the shape *and* structure of a thing. When referring to two-dimensional artworks, it is the visual aspect of composition, structure, and the work as a whole.

FORMAL Traditional and generally accepted visual solutions that are strictly observed.

FRESCO A mural painting technique that uses pigments mixed in water to form the desired color. These pigments are then applied to wet lime plaster, which binds with and becomes an integral part of the wall.

GESTURE A line that does not stay at the edges, but moves freely within forms. These lines record movement of the eye as well as the form.

GOLDEN MEAN A mathematical ratio in which width is to length as length is to length plus width. This ratio has been employed in design since the ancient Greeks. It can also be found in natural forms.

GOLDEN RECTANGLE The ancient Greek ideal of a perfectly proportioned rectangle using a mathematical ratio called the *Golden Mean.*

GRAPHIC Forms drawn or painted onto a two-dimensional surface. Any illustration or design.

GRID A network of horizontal and vertical intersecting lines that divide spaces and create a framework of areas.

GROUND The surface of a two-dimensional design that acts as the background for the "figures" in the composition. The ground orients the viewer in space by the contrasts and relationships that exist with the figure.

HIERATIC SCALE A composition in which the size of figures is determined by their thematic importance.

HORIZON LINE The farthest point we can see where the delineation between the sky and ground becomes distinct. The line on the picture plane that indicates the extent of illusionistic space and on which are located the vanishing points.

HUE A property of color defined by distinctions within the visual spectrum or color wheel.

IDEALISM An artistic theory in which the world is not reproduced as it is, but as it should be. All flaws, accidents, and incongruities of the visual world are corrected.

ILLUSTRATION A picture created to clarify or accompany a text.

IMBALANCE Occurs when opposing or interacting forms are out of equilibrium in a pictorial composition.

IMPASTO A painting technique in which pigments are applied in thick layers or strokes in order to create a rough three-dimensional paint surface on the two-dimensional surface.

IMPLIED LINE An invisible line created by positioning a series of points in order to compel the eye to connect them and thus create movement across the picture plane.

IMPRESSIONISM An artistic style that sought to recreate the artist's perception of the changing quality of light and color in nature.

INFORMAL BALANCE Synonymous with asymmetrical balance. It implies a less rigid, more casual balance.

INSTALLATION A mixed media artwork that generally takes into account the environment in which it is arranged.

INTENSITY The saturation of hue perceived in a color.

ISOMETRIC PROJECTION A spatial illusion that occurs when lines receding on the diagonal remain parallel instead of converging towards a common vanishing point. Used commonly in Oriental and Far Eastern art.

JUXTAPOSITION When one image or shape is placed next to or in comparison to another image or shape.

KINESTHETIC EMPATHY A mental process in which the viewer consciously recreates an action or motion he or she observes.

KINETIC Artworks that actually move or have moving parts.

LEGATO A connecting and flowing rhythm.

LINE A visual element of length. It can be created by setting a point in motion.

LINE QUALITY Any one of a number of characteristics of line determined by its weight, direction, uniformity or other features.

LINEAR PERSPECTIVE A spatial system used in two-dimensional artworks to create the illusion of space. It is based on the perception that if parallel lines are extended to the horizon line, they appear to converge and meet at a common point, called the vanishing point.

LINES OF FORCE Lines that add a strong visual emphasis to a particular motion.

LOCAL COLOR The identifying color perceived in ordinary daylight.

LOST-AND-FOUND CONTOUR A description of a form in which an object is revealed by distinct contours in some areas while other edges simply vanish or dissolve into the ground.

MANDALA A radial concentric organization of geometric shapes and images commonly used in Hindu and Buddhist art.

MEDIUM The tools or materials used to create an artwork.

MINIMALISM An artistic style that stresses purity of form above content and other extraneous or trivial elements.

MIXED MEDIA The combination of two or more different mediums in a single work of art.

MODULE A specific measured area or standard unit.

MONOCHROMATIC A color scheme using only one hue with varying degrees of value or intensity.

MULTIPLE IMAGE A visual device to suggest movement that occurs when a figure is in a sequence of slightly overlapping poses in which each successive position suggests movement from the prior position.

NATURALISM The skillful representation of the visual image, forms and proportions as seen in nature with an illusion of volume and three-dimensional space.

NEGATIVE SPACE Unoccupied areas or empty space surrounding the objects or figures in a composition.

NONOBJECTIVE A type of artwork with absolutely no reference to reality.

OBJECTIVE Having to do with reality and fidelity to perception.

ONE-POINT PERSPECTIVE A system of spatial illusion in two-dimensional art based on the convergence of parallel lines to a common vanishing point usually on the horizon.

OPAQUE A surface impenetrable by light.

OPEN FORM The placement of objects in a composition so that they imply completion beyond the boundary of the design.

OVERLAPPING A device for creating an illusion of depth in which some shapes partially hide or obscure others.

PATTERN The repetition of a visual element or module in a regular and anticipated sequence

PICTURE PLANE The two-dimensional surface on which shapes are organized into a composition.

PLANE The two-dimensional surface of a shape.

POINTILLISM A system of color mixing based on the juxtaposition of small bits of pure color. Also called Divisionism.

Pop Art An art movement originating in the 1960s that sought inspiration from everyday popular culture and the techniques of commercial art.

Positive Shape Any shape or object distinguished from the background.

Primary Colors The three colors from which all other colors can theoretically be mixed. The primaries of pigments are traditionally presented as red, yellow, and blue, while the primaries of light are red, blue, and green.

Progressive Rhythm Repetition of shape that changes in a regular pattern.

Proportion Size measured against other elements or against a mental norm or standard. A ratio.

Proximity The degree of closeness.

Psychic Line A mental connection between two points or elements. This occurs when a figure is pointing or looking in a certain direction which causes the eye to follow towards the intended focus.

Radial Balance A composition in which all visual elements are balanced around a central point.

Realism An approach to artwork based on the faithful reproduction of surface appearances with a fidelity to visual perception.

Rectilinear Composed of straight lines.

Repeated Figure A compositional device in which a recognizable figure appears within the same composition in different positions and situations so as to relate a narrative to the viewer.

Repetition Using the same visual element over again within the same composition.

Representational An image suggestive of an object which actually exists.

Rhythm An element of design based on the repetition of recurrent motifs.

Saturation See Intensity.

Secondary Color A mixture of any two primary colors.

Shade A hue mixed with black.

Shape A visually perceived area created either by an enclosing line or by color and value changes defining the outer edges.

Silhouette The area between the contours of a shape.

Simultaneous Contrast The effect created by two colors seen in juxtaposition.

Site Specific A work of art in which the content and aesthetic value is dependent on the artwork's location.

Spectrum The range of visible color created when white light is passed through a prism.

Staccato Abrupt changes and dynamic contrast within the visual rhythm.

Subject The content of an artwork.

Subjective Reflecting a personal bias.

Subtractive System A color mixing system in which pigment (physical substance) is combined to create visual sensations of color. Wavelengths of light absorbed by the substance are subtracted and the reflected wavelengths constitute the perceived color.

Surrealism An artistic style that stresses fantastic and subconscious approaches to art making and often results in images that cannot be rationally explained.

Symbol An element of design that communicates an idea or meaning beyond that of its literal form.

Symmetry A quality of a composition or form wherein there is a precise correspondence of elements that reference to an axis or a point.

Tactile Texture The use of actual materials to create a surface that can actually be felt or touched.

Tertiary A mixture of a primary and an adjacent secondary color.

Texture The surface quality of objects that appeals to the tactile sense.

Tint A hue mixed with white.

Tone A hue mixed with its complement.

Tonality A single color or hue that dominates the entire color structure despite the presence of other colors.

Translucent A situation in which objects, forms, or planes transmit and diffuse light but have a degree of opacity that does not allow clear visibility through the form.

Transparency A situation in which an object or form allows light to pass through it.

Triadic A color scheme involving three equally spaced colors on the color wheel.

Trompe l'oeil A French term meaning "to fool the eye." The objects are in sharp focus and delineated with meticulous care to create an artwork that fools the viewer into believing that the images are real.

Unity The degree of agreement existing among the elements in a design.

Value A measure of relative lightness or darkness.

Value Emphasis When a light and dark contrast is used to create a focal point within a composition.

Value Pattern The arrangement and amount of variation in light and dark values independent of any colors used.

Vanishing Point In linear perspective, the point at which parallel lines appear to converge on the horizon line. Depending on the view there may be more than one vanishing point.

Vernacular A prevailing style or attitude in a specific geographical location, group of people, or time period.

Vertical Location A spatial device in which elevation on the page or format indicates a recession into depth. The higher an object, the farther back it is assumed to be.

Vibrating Colors Colors that create a flickering effect at their border. This effect is usually dependent on an equal value relationship and strong hue contrast.

Visual Color Mixing The optical mixture of small units of color so that the eye perceives the mixture rather than the individual component colors.

Visual Texture A two-dimensional illusion suggestive of a tactile quality.

Volume The appearance of height, width and depth in a form.

Warm Color A color that appears to be closer to the yellow to red side of the color wheel.

BIBLIOGRAPHY

GENERAL

Berger, John. *Ways of Seeing*. London: British Broadcast Corporation, 1987.

Canaday, John. *What is Art?* New York: Alfred A. Knopf, 1980.

Dondis, Donis A. *A Primer of Visual Literacy*. Cambridge, MA: MIT Press, 1973.

Faulkner, Ray, Edwin Ziegfeld, and Howard Smagula. *Art Today: An Introduction to the Visual Arts,* 6th ed. Fort Worth, TX: Harcourt Brace College Publishers, 1987.

McCarter, R. William, and Rita Gilbert. *Living with Art,* 2nd ed. New York: McGraw-Hill, Inc., 1988.

Preble, Duane, and Sarah Preble. *Artforms: An Introduction to the Visual Arts,* 5th ed. New York: HarperCollins Publishers, Inc., 1993.

ART HISTORY

Arnason, H. H. *History of Modern Art,* 3rd rev. ed. New York: Harry N. Abrams, Inc., 1986.

Gardner, Louise. *Art Through the Ages.* 9th ed. Orlando, FL: Harcourt Brace College Publishers, 1991.

Janson, H. W. *History of Art,* 4th rev. and enl. ed. New York: Harry N. Abrams, Inc., 1991.

Smagula, Howard. *Currents.* 2nd ed. Englewood Cliffs, NJ: Prentice-Hall, 1989.

GENERAL DESIGN

Bevlin, Marjorie Elliot. *Design through Discovery,* 5th ed. Ft. Worth, TX: Harcourt Brace College Publishers, 1989.

Bothwell, Dorr, and Marlys Frey. *Notan: Dark–Light Principle of Design.* New York: Dover, 1991.

Collier, Graham. *Form, Space and Vision: An Introduction to Drawing and Design,* 4th ed. Englewood Cliffs, NJ: Prentice-Hall, 1985.

De Lucio-Meyer, J. *Visual Aesthetics.* New York: Harper & Row, 1974.

De Sausmarez, Maurice. *Basic Design: The Dynamics of Visual Form.* Blue Ridge Summit, PA: T A B Books, 1990.

Hoffman, Armin. *Graphic Design Manual.* New York: Van Nostrand Reinhold, 1977.

Hurlburt, Allen. *The Design Concept.* New York: Watson-Gupthill Publications, Inc., 1981.

Hurlburt, Allen. *The Grid.* New York: Van Nostrand Reinhold, 1982.

Hurlburt, Allen. *Layout: The Design of the Printed Page.* New York: Watson-Guptill Publications, Inc., 1989.

Itten, Johannes. *Design and Form: The Basic Course at the Bauhaus,* 2nd rev. ed. New York: Van Nostrand Reinhold, 1975.

Kepes, Gyorgy. *Language of Vision.* Chicago: Paul Theobald, 1969.

Kerlow, Isaac Victor, and Judson Rosebush. *Computer Graphics.* New York: Van Nostrand Reinhold, 1986.

Maier, Manfred. *Basic Principles of Design.* New York: Van Nostrand Reinhold, 1977.

Mante, Harald. *Photo Design: Picture Composition for Black and White Photography.* New York: Van Nostrand Reinhold, 1971.

McKim, Robert H. *Thinking Visually.* New York: Van Nostrand Reinhold, 1980.

Myers, Jack Frederick. *The Language of Visual Art.* Orlando, FL: Holt, Rinehart and Winston, 1989.

Stoops, Jack, and Jerry Samuelson. *Design Dialogue.* Worcester, MA: Davis Publications, 1983.

Wilde, Richard. *Problems: Solutions: Visual Thinking for Graphic Communications.* New York: Van Nostrand Reinhold, 1989.

Wong, Wucius. *Principles of Two-Dimensional Design.* New York: Van Nostrand Reinhold, 1972.

Wong, Wucius. *Principles of Three-Dimensional Design.* New York: Van Nostrand Reinhold, 1977.

VISUAL PERCEPTION

Arnheim, Rudolf. *Art and Visual Perception: A Psychology of the Creative Eye, the New Version,* 2nd rev. and enl. ed. Berkeley: University of California Press, 1974.

Bloomer, Carolyn M. *Principles of Visual Perception,* 2nd ed. New York: Van Nostrand Reinhold, 1989.

Ehrenzweig, Anton. *The Hidden Order of Art: A Study in the Psychology of Artistic Imagination.* Berkeley: University of California Press, 1976.

Gombrich, E. H. *Art and Illusion: A Study in the Psychology of Pictorial Representation.* Princeton, NJ: Princeton University Press, 1961.

SPACE

Carraher, Ronald G., and Jacqueline B. Thurston. *Optical Illusions and the Visual Arts.* New York: Van Nostrand Reinhold, 1966.

Coulin, Claudius. *Step-by-Step Perspective Drawing: For Architects, Draftsmen and Designers.* New York: Van Nostrand Reinhold, 1971.

D'Amelio, Joseph. *Perspective Drawing Handbook.* New York: Leon Amiel, Publisher, 1964.

Doblin, Jay. *Perspective: A New System for Designers,* 11th ed. New York: Whitney Library of Design, 1976.

Ivins, William M., Jr. *On the Rationalization of Sight: With an Examination of Three Renaissance Texts on Perspective to Which is Appended ''De Artificiali Perspectiva'' by Viator (Pelerin).* New York: Da Capo Press, Inc., 1973.

Luckiesh, M. *Visual Illusions: Their Causes, Characteristics and Applications.* New York: Dover Publications, 1965.

Montague, John. *Basic Perspective Drawing,* 2nd ed. New York: Van Nostrand Reinhold, 1993.

Mulvey, Frank. *Graphic Perception of Space.* New York: Van Nostrand Reinhold, 1969.

O'Connor, Charles A., Jr. *Perspective Drawing and Applications.* Englewood Cliffs, NJ: Prentice-Hall, 1985.

White, J. *The Birth and Rebirth of Pictorial Space,* 3rd ed. Cambridge, MA: Harvard University Press, 1987.

TEXTURE

Battersby, Marton. *Trompe-l'Oeil: The Eye Deceived.* New York: St. Martin's Press, 1974.

Proctor, Richard M. *The Principles of Pattern: For Craftsmen and Designers.* New York: Van Nostrand Reinhold, 1969.

Wescher, Herta. *Collage.* New York: Harry N. Abrams, 1968.

COLOR

Albers, Josef. *Interaction of Color,* rev. ed. New Haven, CT: Yale University Press, 1975.

Birren, Faber. *Creative Color: A Dynamic Approach for Artists and Designers.* New York: Van Nostrand Reinhold, 1961.

Birren, Faber, ed. *Itten: The Elements of Color.* New York: Van Nostrand Reinhold, 1970.

Birren, Faber, ed. *Munsell: A Grammar of Color.* New York: Van Nostrand Reinhold, 1969.

Birren, Faber. *Ostwald: The Color Primer.* New York: Van Nostrand Reinhold, 1969.

Birren, Faber. *Principles of Color,* rev. ed. West Chester, PA: Schiffer Publishing, Limited, 1987.

De Grandis, Luigina. *Theory and Use of Color.* New York: Harry N. Abrams, Incorporated, 1987.

Fabri, Frank. *Color: A Complete Guide for Artists.* New York: Watson-Guptill, 1967.

Gerritsen, Frank J. *Theory and Practice of Color.* New York: Van Nostrand Reinhold, 1974.

Itten, Johannes. *The Art of Color,* rev. ed. New York: Van Nostrand Reinhold, 1984.

Kippers, Harald. *Color: Origin, Systems, Uses.* New York: Van Nostrand Reinhold, 1973.

Rhode, Ogden N. *Modern Chromatics: The Student's Textbook of Color with Application to Art and Industry,* new ed. New York: Van Nostrand Reinhold, 1973.

Varley, Helen ed. *Color.* Los Angeles: Knapp Press, 1980.

Verity, Enid. *Color Observed.* New York: Van Nostrand Reinhold, 1980.

Zelanski, Paul, and Mary Pat Fisher. *Color.* Englewood Cliffs, NJ: Prentice-Hall, 1989.

PHOTOGRAPHIC SOURCES

The authors and publisher wish to thank the custodians of the works of art for supplying photographs and granting permission to use them. Photographers and sources for photographs other than those listed in the captions are given below.

A/AR: Alinari/Art Resource, New York
AR: Art Resource, New York
FM/AR: Foto Marburg/Art Resource, New York
G/AR: Giraudon/Art Resource, New York
PR: Photo Researchers, New York
RMN: © Cliche Musees Nationaux/Service de Documentation Photographique de la Reunion des Musees Nationaux, Paris
S/AR: Scala/Art Resource, New York
TG/AR: Tate Gallery, London/Art Resource, New York

Cover and title page: Jack Zeman, Dallas.

Chapter 1 Opener: Eva Hesse Studio, detail, 1966. Installation photograph by Gretchen Lambert. © The Estate of Eva Hesse. All rights reserved. (3a) © 1983 John Kuchera. (8a and 8b) Raymond Loewy, *Industrial Design,* Woodstock, NY: Overlook Press; Copyright © 1988 Raymond Loewy. (9d) Kevin Fitzsimons. (10a) © 1993 Frank Wing. (11c) D. James Dee. (14b) © 1983 Dan Budnik/Woodfin Camp & Associates. (14c) © Dan Budnik/Woodfin Camp & Associates. (15d and 15e) Raymond Loewy International Group Ltd., London.

Chapter 2 Opener: Alex Katz. *Black Jacket,* detail, 1972. Oil on aluminum (cutout), 62⅝ × 36¼″ (159 × 92 cm). Des Moines Art Center (gift in honor of Mrs. E. T. Meredith, Permanent Collection, 1978.7). (23e) Richard Frieman/PR. (27b) Collection David Reynolds. (28d) RMN. (34a) Copyright © Alan Bowness. (34b) Harold Dorwin. (35c) © 1984 Kenneth A. Hannon.

Chapter 3 Opener: Maurice Utrillo. *Church of Le Sacre Coeur, Montmartre et rue Saint-Rustique,* detail. N.d. Oil on canvas, 19⅝ × 24″ (50 × 61 cm). Courtesy, Museum of Fine Arts, Boston (bequest of John T. Spaulding). (44a) G/AR. (45b) Superstock. (47c) David Stansburg. (50c) TG/AR.

Chapter 4 Opener: Eugeniusz Get-Staniewicz. *Self-Portrait,* detail. 1980. Reproduced from:

"Design in Poland," *Print* magazine, May/June 1992, p. 67. Courtesy of *Print.* (56a) Fredrik Marsh. (57b) National Museum of American Art, Washington, DC/AR. (57c) G/AR. (58b) G/AR. (59d) © 1993 Rob Lewine. (62b) © Canali Photobank, Capriolo, Italy. (68b) A/AR. (69c) A/AR.

Chapter 5 Opener: Suzuki Harunobu. *Girl with Lantern on Balcony at Night,* detail. Ca. 1768. Color woodcut, 12¾ × 8¼″ (32 × 21 cm). Metropolitan Museum of Art, New York (Fletcher Fund, 1929; JP 150). Photo: Ken Burris. (76b) © 1983 Steve Rosenthal. (77c) A/AR. (78a) A/AR. (79b) Kevin Fitzsimons. (81b) © 1988 Paul Warchol, New York. (83d) RMN. (90a) G/AR.

Chapter 6 Opener: Le Corbusier. Unite d'Habitation, detail. 1947–1952. External escape stairway, Marseilles. © ESTO/Ezra Stoller. (98a) © 1976 Bruce Barnbaum. (100a) © ESTO/Ezra Stoller. (102a) Art Alanis.

Chapter 7 Opener: Susan Rothenberg. *Untitled,* detail. 1978. Acrylic, flashe, pencil on paper, 20 × 20″ (51 × 51 cm). Collection Walker Art Center, Minneapolis (Art Center Acquisition Fund, 1979). (110c) © Norman McGrath. (115d) Sovfoto, New York. (122a) © Jim Strong, Inc. (122b) A/AR. (126a) RMN.

Chapter 8 Opener: Theo van Doesburg. *Composition IX, Opus 18 (Card Players),* detail. 1917. Oil on canvas, 45¼ × 41⅜″ (116 × 106 cm). Gemeentemuseum, The Hague. (130a) Courtesy Brod Gallery, London. (130b) TG/AR. (132a) Bernd Kirtz. (133b) D. James Dee. (133c) © 1990 Frederik Marsh. (135b) FM/AR. (135c) Geoffrey Clements. (137b) A/AR. (137c) Sovfoto, New York. (139b) Catalogue no. 33118, photo no. 83-10907, Dept. of Anthropology, Smithsonian Institution. (140a) Reprinted from: Sarabianov and Adaskina, *Popova,* 1990; St. Petersburg: Aurora Press. (140b) George Holmes. (145d) Laurin McCracken. (146d) RMN.

Chapter 9 Opener: Lawrence Walker. *The Horn,* detail. Mixed media. Vicki Prentice Associates, Inc., Los Angeles. (153b) © ESTO/Ezra Stoller. (154a) G/AR. (160a) Adam Reich. (161d) © 1983 Peter Mauss. (162a) F. Schumacher & Co.

Chapter 10 Opener: Ingo Swann. *Highways I,* detail. 1976. Oil on canvas, 40 × 40″ (102 × 102 cm). National Air and Space Museum, Smithsonian Institution (gift of the artist). (166a) Robert Burley/Design Archive. (171d) Reprinted from: E. H. Gombrich, *Art and Illusion* by permission of Phaidon Press, London. (177d) RMN. (192a) RMN. (193c) Andrew Moore.

Chapter 11 Opener: Thomas Eakins. *Man Pole-Vaulting,* detail. Ca. 1884. Photograph. Metropolitan Museum of Art, New York (gift of Charles Bregler, 1941; 41.142.11).

Chapter 12 Opener: James McNeill Whistler. *At the Piano,* detail. 1858–59. Oil on canvas, 26⅜ × 36¹/₁₆″ (67 × 92 cm). Taft Museum, Cincinnati (bequest of Louise Taft Semple, 1962.7). (214b) A/AR. (218a) A/AR. (220c) FM/AR.

Chapter 13 Opener: Henri Matisse. *Portrait of Mme. Matisse,* detail. 1905. Oil on canvas, 16 × 12⅞″ (40.5 × 32.5 cm). Statens Museum for Kunst, Copenhagen. (226a) G/AR. (226b) Erich Lessing/AR. (233d) S/AR. (234a) John Back. (247e) J. Kevin Fitzsimons. (250b) David Reynolds.

Illustration copyrights: Artists Rights Society, New York, and Visual Artists and Galleries Association, Inc., New York:

Copyright 1995 ARS/ADAGP: 116b, 208c, 240a, 240b, 243c. Copyright 1995 ARS/ADAGP/SPADEM: 50c, 159b, 233d. Copyright 1995 ARS/SPADEM: 28c, 123d, 149c, 250a. Copyright 1995 ARS/VG Bild-Kunst, Bonn: 26a, 74b, 80a, 126c, 126d, 168a. Copyright 1995 Fernando Botero/VAGA: 45c. Copyright 1995 Estate of Stuart Davis/VAGA: 43b, 254a, 255b. Copyright 1995 Estate of Theo van Doesburg/VAGA: Ch. 8 Opener, 143c. Copyright 1995 Estate of James Ensor/VAGA: 45b. Copyright 1995 Estate of David Smith/VAGA: 132a. Copyright 1995 Agnes Fielding/ARS: 139c. Copyright 1995 C. Hersocovici/ARS: 66a, 196b. Copyright 1995 Alex Katz/VAGA: Ch. 2 Opener, 19c. Copyright 1995 Georgia O'Keeffe Foundation/ARS: 236a. Copyright 1995 Willem de Kooning/ARS: 200b, 233c. Copyright 1995 Robert Rauschenberg/VAGA: 33e. Copyright 1995 Succession H. Matisse/ARS: 115d, 220b, Ch. 13 Opener, 249b.

INDEX